"An eloquent, timely, well researched and pov
impact of porn on our culture. Further, it adds
a major public health problem. Every parent ʻ

Part of the power of this book is it tells the stoʻy oʻ many who struggle. Porn U makes clear this is not just about men or desire; rather it speaks to all of us and our future."

Dr. Patrick Carnes, Ph.D.
Author of *Out of the Shadows: Understanding Sexual Addiction*

------------------------------ ☒ ☒ ☒ ------------------------------

"Michael Leahy is a man on a mission to help college students ask the hard questions about the pornified culture we live in. Leahy has his finger on the sexual pulse of the American campus like no one else today. *Porn University* is a startling and deadly accurate picture of how porn is affecting the life of young adults today."

Lynn McClurg
VP, Director of Marketing, Covenant Eyes

------------------------------ ☒ ☒ ☒ ------------------------------

"There simply is no other issue that has such far-reaching social and spiritual ramifications and Michael Leahy is one of few individuals qualified to speak to it. No one has more intimate knowledge and understanding of the effects, the industry, the victims, and how pornography will affect and influence the next and newest generations. This is the true story of pornography."

Rick James
Publisher, CruPress Campus Crusade for Christ; author of *Jesus Without Religion*

------------------------------ ☒ ☒ ☒ ------------------------------

"The new book by Michael Leahy, *Porn University*, gets right at the heart of a growing epidemic on our college campuses. In a search for intimacy, men and women are looking for 'love in all the wrong places.' I appreciate Michael's honesty and the hope he gives for freedom from the addiction of pornography. I highly recommend his book."

Earle J. Chute
Campus Crusade for Christ staff member for 35 years.

--------------------------- X X X ------------------------------

"Michael is an expert when it comes to the sexuality of our times. His experience personally with the destructive nature of porn, and the fresh insights he has gained from today's college student, more than qualifies him to speak to the sobering realities and consequences of our 'sex everywhere' culture."

Bob Francis
National Director for Campus Field Strategies, Campus Crusade for Christ

--------------------------- X X X ------------------------------

"Michael Leahy is not only an expert on college student sexuality but a courageous and authentic voice with a powerful story of redemption and hope. Spoken with both truth and compassion, *Porn University* is a must read for students who desire sexual and relational wholeness."

Nick DeCola
Member Care Coordinator, Campus Crusade for Christ

--------------------------- X X X ------------------------------

"*Porn University* gives startling insights into today's hypersexual campus culture. After visiting over 100 campuses, Michael Leahy understands what is happening in students' lives and offers hope for healthy, lasting change. *Porn University* is a must read."

Tony Arnold
Media Relations Director, Campus Crusade for Christ

---------------------------- X X X ----------------------------

"This generation of college students is hungrier and thirstier than any I've seen in twenty-five years of campus ministry. Michael Leahy soberly quantifies for us the amount of porn it's consuming—in its ravenous search for true bread and living water."

Daniel Curran
Campus Crusade for Christ, Bay Area Campus Ministries

---------------------------- X X X ----------------------------

"Wow, what a transparent look at a life and a generation inundated with Porn. It's like a flashing *Danger* sign with life lines attached!"

Michael Woodard
National Director University Ministry, Campus for Christ, Canada

---------------------------- X X X ----------------------------

PORN UNIVERSITY

XXX

WHAT COLLEGE STUDENTS ARE REALLY SAYING ABOUT SEX ON CAMPUS

MICHAEL LEAHY

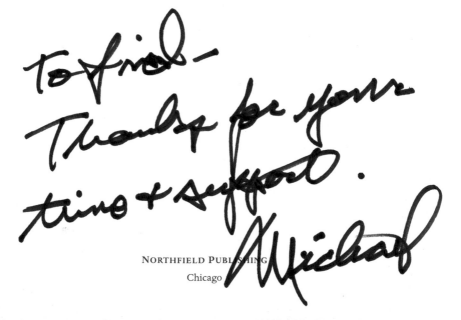

To Fred —
Thanks for you're
time + support.

Michael

NORTHFIELD PUBLISHING

Chicago

© 2009 by
MICHAEL LEAHY

All Web sites listed herein are accurate at the time of publication, but may change in the future or cease to exist. The listing of Web site references and resources does not imply publisher endorsement of the site's entire contents. Groups, corporations, and organizations are listed for informational purposes, and listing does not imply publisher endorsement of their activities.

Published in association with the literary and editorial agencies of Credo Communications, Inc., 16778 S.E. Cohiba Ct., Damascus, OR 97089, www.sanfordci.com

Cover design: DesignWorks Group
Cover image: iStockphoto
Interior design: Smartt Guys design
Editor: Christopher Reese

Library of Congress Cataloging-in-Publication Data

Leahy, Michael.
Porn university : what college students are really saying about sex on campus / Michael Leahy.
    p. cm.
Includes bibliographical references.
ISBN 978-0-8024-8128-3
1. College students--Sexual behavior. 2. College students--Attitudes. 3. Pornography--United States. 4. Sex addiction--United States. 5. Sex in mass media--United States. I. Title.
HQ35.2.L43 2009
176'.708420973--dc22

                    2008052457

This book is printed on acid free recycled paper containing 30% PCW (Post Consumer Waste) and manufactured in the United States of America by Bethany Press.

We hope you enjoy this book from Northfield Publishing. Our goal is to provide high-quality, thought-provoking books and products that connect truth to your real needs and challenges. For more information on other books and products written and produced from a biblical perspective, go to www.moodypublishers.com or write to:

Northfield Publishing
820 N. LaSalle Boulevard
Chicago, IL 60610

1 3 5 7 9 10 8 6 4 2

Printed in the United States of America

This book is dedicated to my two boys, Christopher and Andrew

To Christopher, my firstborn and college student,
your future is now and this is your truth:

You are God's child.
You are a leader.
Your gift is integrity.
Your pursuit is righteousness.
Your heart is strong.
You inspire others.
They see your courage.
They see Jesus in your smile.
God is glorified through your passion.
The revolution is yours to start,
But whatever you choose to do in life,
You will *always* have His love and mine.

And to Andrew, my youngest and junior high student,
your future is tomorrow and this is your truth:

You are God's child.
You are a leader.
Your gift is loving-kindness.
Your pursuit is justice.
Your heart is tender.
You comfort others.
They see your peace and joy.
They see Jesus in your eyes.
God is glorified through your compassion.
The revolution is yours to grow,
But whatever you choose to do in life,
You will *always* have His love and mine.

CONTENTS

Introduction 11

PART 1: PORN U: PORN NATION'S MECCA

1. Back to School 19

2. Am I a Sex Addict? 31

3. The Sexual Addiction Screening Test 39

PART 2: AND THE SURVEY SAID . . .

4. A Quick Look at Demographics 47

5. First Exposure: Men Are from Mars, and 53

6. Students Behaving Badly: Porn U's Walking Wounded 63

7. Sex on the Brain 73

8. So How's That Working for You? 83

9. Who's in Control Here? 95

10. From Sex Syndrome to Sex Addiction 105

PART 3: GRADUATE STUDIES

11. Being Known or Being Noticed? 117

12. What Every Student *Really* Wants—and Needs 127

13. A Letter from Dad 137

Conclusion: How to Start a Revolution 143

Appendix: SAST Survey Results 151

Notes 161

Acknowledgments 165

About the Author 169

INTRODUCTION

We've all heard the expression "Never judge a book by its cover." Well, this could very well be one of those books. The kind of book that surprises its reader at every turn. I like reading books like that. I like writing them even better.

For instance, I'm not sure what first came to mind when you read the title of this book. Maybe you work with college students and you thought, "Porn University! Okay, I wonder what these profligate students are into now?" Or maybe you're a parent who was thinking, "What!? As if I don't have enough to worry about trying to raise kids in this crazy world of ours." Perhaps you're a college student who was rolling your eyes and bracing for the worst: "Great! That's all we need—another book from some self-righteous morality junkie telling the world how awful and messed up we are."

Well, this book isn't any of those things. In fact, I think you'll be just as pleasantly surprised as I was while doing the research. That experience proved to me once again that things aren't always quite as they seem. Especially when the topic involves college students and you start getting to know who they really are by having honest, gut-wrenching conversations with them like I have these past several years. It doesn't take long before you find them peeling back the layers of those protective covers they've so meticulously woven around themselves to try to conceal who they really are. Letting others see who we really are and revealing what we've been hiding for so long can be a frightening experience. Unfortunately, that fear usually wins out in the end for most of us, and we continue to keep our lives hidden and remain mostly unknown to others, and even ourselves.

I should know. I was a master of disguise, adept at wearing many masks in order to keep the truth about me from seeping out—playing alternating characters throughout my life like the popular student athlete, the loyal husband, the compassionate family man, the busy and important corporate executive. Yet underneath it all I was really just an average guy struggling to keep it all together while fighting a growing obsession with sex and pornography. I know all too well the lies we weave and the games we play with ourselves and others just to keep a secret, just to stay hidden. For that reason, in writing this book about the sexual attitudes, beliefs, and behaviors of college students, I've tried to be more the observer than the judge and critic. As any of my fellow recovering addicts will tell you, those of us who live in glass houses realize we have no business throwing stones at others. If anything, I'm just a guy who's the product of a whole lot of undeserved grace and mercy extended to me by others, and certainly by God. I learned some hard lessons about the value of openness and honesty and transparency in relationships, but not until my lack of these qualities cost me a fifteen-year marriage and my family and a budding business partnership, just to name a few.

What I have learned these past several years after being around college students and having one of my own on campus is the high degree of importance they place on authenticity and vulnerability. We know those two elements are critical in creating a safe environment for honest sharing and healthy intimacy with others, both inside and outside of recovery groups. So when it comes to openly discussing with others such sensitive subjects as love, sex, relationships, and porn, there is no room for judgment and condemnation, including self-condemnation. These only serve to choke openness and mask wounds. Rather, in this context, facts are friendly and authenticity is king!

For these reasons, I plan on employing the same approach in this book that I use in speaking with students as we examine the sexual attitudes, beliefs, and behaviors of today's college students. In what follows, we're going to examine what college students are *really* saying about sex on campus and in their private lives. But in their own words and based on their own self-reflection. This book is not an indictment of college students and their sexual morality or immorality, but rather a closer look at how they see themselves as sexual beings. There's a big difference in those two approaches, and reporting on someone's self-assessment is something I believe we don't do often enough. After all, let's face it—even though we all look pretty normal on the outside, that's seldom the case once you get to know us. It's what is going on in the inside that really matters, right? I mean, there's a lot more to our story than most people realize, and I don't think there's a soul on the planet who wouldn't like to be better understood and truly known by others. The students I've been talking to over the past five years overwhelmingly feel that way. If you do too, then this book is definitely for you.

The centerpiece of *Porn University*'s exploration of the sexuality of today's college students is the result of an online sex survey I've been conducting over the past several years in conjunction with my college speaking tours. But what makes this unique and especially interesting are two key factors: first, it's a MASSIVE study by any measure. In an era of exit polling and quick surveys involving a few hundred people or so, we've surveyed over twenty-six thousand college and university students. That makes this arguably the largest unofficial and informal study of its kind ever conducted on a single demographic group. Second, this wasn't just your typical makeshift sex survey asking a few questions like, "How often do you have sex?" or "Have you ever had an STD?" Twenty-five of the thirty-three-questions we asked in our sex survey come directly from a widely used, early diagnostic screening test called the Sexual Addiction Screening Test (or SAST for short). The SAST was developed by Dr. Patrick Carnes, a pioneer and one of the world's leading medical experts in the field of sexual addiction and recovery. The test is used extensively by health care professionals and clinicians as well as individual patients. In our case, with Dr. Carnes's permission, we invited students to go online and take a standardized version of the SAST that we developed (www.mysexsurvey.com) as a self-guided, diagnostic test. We just never expected so many students to take us up on the offer.

This ongoing study is groundbreaking in many respects, as you'll see from the early findings that I'll be discussing in this book. I say "early" because due to the massive size and unique nature of the responses we've received, it may take some time before we have completely analyzed and fully understand the ramifications of the data and findings we've collected. Yet, just as important as the results of this history-making study are some of the comments and personal stories coming from the students themselves that I have interspersed throughout the book. They're a small sampling of the thousands upon thousands of written comments I've received and verbal conversations I've had with students around the country as they elaborate on their own personal stories. While statistics can only provide us with numerical representations of real life, nothing stirs the soul and the spirit quite like the words that flow out of the human heart—words that attempt to convey meaning and understanding to others. Very often I've noticed these same students voicing a deeper desire for connection and community. And it all makes sense. We are, after all, highly relational beings. In one way or another, we all need each other. And that never became clearer to me than when I started reading the comments and hearing the personal stories coming from the students I met during my campus speaking events and in the process of collecting this data.

This generation of students and their place in history is unique and so important to us. Their stories need to be told, not just for their sake, but for ours as well. They share lessons some of us need to learn and others we need to be reminded of. Without hearing what they have to say, it's too easy for us to forget about our own past and the part of us that we see in them—reminding us that we're all interconnected in the collective human experience.

Finally, I'll close with some thoughts and ideas on a rather interesting phenomenon I've been noticing as I've observed college students over the years. As I've spoken all over the country and around the world, I've challenged my student audiences to consider the connection that many believe exists between sexuality and spirituality.[1] Both are considered to be a measure of intimacy, one mainly existing in the physical realm and experienced between two people, the other mainly existing in the spiritual realm and experienced between a person and God. While most of the students I've spoken with have had a lot to say about this subject and certainly represent a wide array of viewpoints, one thing that everyone could agree on in the end was that one of *our greatest needs as human beings is not to be loved, but to love others*, even if we don't necessarily feel like we are doing a very good job of it. For many, like myself, that wasn't self-evident at first. Life was much more about taking rather than giving for a very long time. As a result, my life was often characterized by a very empty and shallow existence that left me wanting for more without really knowing what it was I really wanted. Thus, there's a lot for us to think about as we read this book. Because it's not really just about how college students perceive and pursue love, sex, and relationships with others. It's also about how we *all* are on a journey to recognize what our deepest needs and desires are and to discover healthy and deeply satisfying ways to meet them. In fact, as I and many others have discovered in our own lives—often after trying everything else—our deepest needs are ultimately met through a spiritual connection with God that takes place when we place our faith in His Son Jesus Christ. This kind of self-awareness and spiritual revelation is almost always part of the stories I hear from today's college students who are living abundant, deeply satisfying lives.

Because the lessons we learn in *Porn University* are so multifaceted and interdependent, I don't think this book will fit nicely into whatever category you had in mind when you looked at the cover. But that is also true of today's college student—hard to define, harder still to label, yet just like the rest of us so hungry deep down to be fully known by others. My hope is that through their confessions of their inner lives and the ways they think of themselves as sexual beings, we will be inspired to embrace the truth that we were all created for relationship and to love one another in ways that elevate our common humanity. A truly revolutionary idea for today's Porn Universities.

PART ONE

PORN U:
PORN NATION'S MECCA

CHAPTER 1

BACK TO SCHOOL

As an activist of sorts on the subject of pornography and the sexualization of our culture, I'm often asked, "Why do you speak mainly to college students? Shouldn't you be spending more time talking about this with younger kids?" It's a good question; since the average age of first exposure to porn is twelve to thirteen years of age (and falling), it would seem to make more sense for me to target preteens with my message about the hidden dangers and long-term consequences of porn consumption. But while on the surface this might seem more logical, the truth is I speak more often to college students than I do to any other demographic group because that's where I was when what eventually became my thirty-year relationship with porn started to escalate. Like many college students today, I wasn't just a casual consumer of porn. I was one of the industry's biggest fans! For that reason, I think my strongest audience connection has been and always will be with college students.

I was eleven years old when I was first exposed to porn. Porn fascinated me. I liked it a lot. Even though the material was not nearly as accessible then as it is today, I diligently stayed on the lookout for it. But there was a small obstacle keeping me from openly pursuing my passion for porn—my parents. Like most preteens, I lived under my parents' roof and would continue to do so throughout high school. They were the lawgivers, and I never had to guess how they might have felt about my perusing a *Playboy* or *Penthouse* magazine here or there: I fully expected that my life as I knew it would cease to exist! In fact, the whole subject of sex was pretty much off-limits in our home, or so I thought.

Therefore, like most of my peers, I ogled over the images in secret. Whatever porn I found lying out in the woods or carelessly tossed in the neighbor's garbage, I confiscated it and kept it in secret stashes well hidden from others. That's part of what made it all so exciting to me back then. The danger, the intrigue. Maybe those were also the early seeds of what would later blossom into a pretty large dose of teenage rebellion. Of course, most of my friends didn't care one way or the other about my use of porn. It was expected and all of the guys did it, or so it seemed to me. But since the risks of getting caught were just too great compared to the hassle of finding and hiding the stuff, more socially acceptable pursuits started to take up the majority of my time—sports, hanging out with friends, and family activities. Porn would go on the back burner until it became easier to access and hide, and before it would take center stage in my life again.

OPPORTUNITY KNOCKS

As it turned out, my friends and I wouldn't have to wait all that long. Once I got to college, porn was the norm in campus life. I attended Eastern Washington University, a small liberal arts school just outside of my hometown of Spokane, Washington. As a student athlete recruited to play football, I arrived in midsummer of 1976. It didn't take me long to realize that while there would still be teachers, administrators, and other adult authority figures I'd have to contend with, porn was generally seen as no big deal. Living in the dorms and later off campus was a far different environment than being at home. From the standpoint of living out my porn-inspired sexual beliefs, I was free—free at last!

Life in the dorms was pretty wide-open sexually back then too, much like it is now. Of course, that doesn't mean it was a nonstop orgy like stories I'd heard about campus life at some colleges during the sexual revolution of the late '60s. But no one seemed to care much if you had a "visitor" stay the night in your room (except for maybe your roommate). For the most part, as long as no one got hurt, we figured you could do whatever you wanted to sexually. And the porn that was our inspiration, our blueprint of human sexuality, flowed just as freely as the sex it inspired. While we didn't have *Playboy* magazines lying around in the common areas of the dorms, they were prevalent behind closed doors. Once I moved out of the dorms into off-campus housing, porn was THE status symbol for independent male living. Having porn magazines and videos lying around in plain sight was compelling evidence that we had cut the cord from Mom and Dad and were on our own, that we were truly adults now fully capable of legally enjoying adult entertainment. Of course, they were temporarily replaced by *Field and Stream* whenever our parents paid a visit.

Going to college amid this newfound sexual liberation and freedom was intoxicating. Not just because of the communal nature of our environment, but also because we could pursue a hedonistic lifestyle with a total lack of accountability. We found ourselves wrapped in this cocoon of relative protection from the outside world while at the same time free from the inquiring eyes of our parents and other authority figures who might be wondering what we were up to.

Of course, that world suited me just fine. I studied hard, played harder, and experienced life pretty much on my own terms. The influence of my parents and the values and social mores of their generation were quickly abandoned and replaced by those of my own and my peers'. Throughout my life, pornography and the remnants of the sexual revolution of the late '60s—my older siblings' generation—had a great impact on me. What I didn't realize was that it also played a key role in the formation of my sexual belief system. In college, I was able to live those beliefs out loud, unencumbered by what other people thought of me or whether or not they judged me. I was my own man now, living by my own rules. As a result, memories of my college days are punctuated with recollections of all-night parties, plenty of drinking and drugging, and a lot of casual sex and one-night stands. Always thinking about having sex. Doing it. Fantasizing about it. Then thinking about it some more. Some would say this sexual exploration and experimentation is an understandable rite of passage at that age, but for me it was always about far more than that. It was also about filling a deeper need for connection, about feeling wanted and accepted. Yet I never sought those things out in the context of a committed relationship. That just sounded like too much work to me. Casual sex, on the other hand, was easy. Especially in college. For me college was all about variety and playing the field and sexual conquests. It's what most guys I hung out with back then were all about—sex as a type of collegiate sport. And yes, it's true. A lot of us even kept score.

At the same time, many of the women I remember in college seemed like they were on a quest of their own. Some appeared motivated by finding true love during their college years, but most that I knew were all about making friends, getting a degree, and having fun along the way, which included having sex. Friendships on campus came easily, and the opportunities were endless. Then there were the friends who offered something extra, often referred to today as "friends with benefits"—girls and guys who were willing to have casual sex with no emotional or relational strings attached. At least that's what we tried to do. In the end a lot of feelings inevitably got hurt, so there seemed to be a lot more students who were into one-night stands than into ongoing "friends with benefits" arrangements.

In the years that followed, I continued to consume porn and pursue sex as a recreational sport. But soon sex was less about recreation and more about satisfying the growing sexual urges I had developed. For instance, getting together with friends after work was never really about just being with friends. There was always an underlying plan to get away at some point in the evening so I could go out and score. I'd troll the bar scene, always on the lookout for a woman whom I thought might sleep with me that night. To go home alone was to end the night in bitter defeat. Disappointed, yet motivated to do better the next time around, it became a game of maintaining emotional equilibrium. My belief was that I had worked hard and was entitled to some fun, even if it came at another person's expense. I still wasn't really looking for a committed, lasting relationship. I was mainly just looking for sex. I needed it to feel a sense of worth and significance, to feel good about myself and who I was. To be a real man in the way I always saw real men portrayed in porn. That was my ideal, to become fulfilled and satisfied as a sexual conqueror of women.

Meeting the woman who would later become my wife was never my plan. It just kind of happened. I was out at a bar with some friends, doing my usual routine of scoping out the dance floor looking for prospects, when I accidentally bumped into Patty. I was living in Seattle at the time but attending a sales training class in Atlanta, and she certainly looked the part of the modern-day Southern belle to me. One dance led to another, and one date led to many more, until I found myself standing at the altar one day getting married. We were definitely in love so getting married seemed like the right thing to do. The only problem was that my desire for a pornographic lifestyle hadn't really abated all that much. If anything, the stress and strain of the next few years of married life only increased my desire to pursue the "Great Escape" of my youth, that being masturbating to pornography in secret. When the stress or pressure would start to build up, or the boredom of my life would settle in, I would turn to my mood-altering drug to rescue me from the trials and tribulations of life and the emotional ups and downs of a real, committed relationship.

Many years and two children later, while still secretly using pornography, I discovered a new world of porn on the Internet while at work as a salesman in the computer industry. Suddenly, I found myself rapidly falling into a black hole of sorts with no defined limits on what kind of porn or how much I could see and experience. As was my custom, I indulged. And I quickly started to lose control. Eventually, even Internet porn didn't offer enough to keep me sufficiently interested and aroused. By now, my thought life was increasingly wrapped up in sexual thoughts and fantasies. Affair scenarios involving other women seemed to pop up constantly. By the time a real woman walked into my office one day and started flirting with me and making advances, I was an affair waiting to happen.

By the time she and I had exchanged a few flirtatious phone conversations and business meetings, I was well on my way to having an affair. Several months after it began, I confessed it to my wife, who was already beginning to suspect that something wasn't right. Eighteen months later, after what could only be described as an all-consuming, totally self-absorbed, increasingly compulsive and addictive relationship with this other woman, I divorced my wife of fifteen years and broke up our family of two boys.[1] I also lost my job and an opportunity at a promising business partnership with my brother. Friends and family soon abandoned me as well, and disappearing with them was my reputation and sense of self-worth.

Eventually, I gave up on my affair partner after discovering that she was also sleeping with at least five other guys who were also married and had families. I had gotten exactly what I deserved, and ironically enough, just what I was looking for—the kind of woman you find portrayed in porn. It had been a year since my divorce when I made this discovery. By then, my ex-wife had found somebody else as well, and not believing that I would ever change, was truly moving on with her life. I hit rock bottom around that time and even became suicidal as I started to wake up to the reality of the consequences I had invited into my life. That was about ten years ago. While I had achieved many of the goals and dreams I had set for my life back when I was a college student—a successful career, a wonderful marriage and family, lots of friends, a comfortable lifestyle living in the suburbs—I had somehow traded it all in for a lie and still wasn't sure how I could have been so stupid, so ignorant, so blind and unaware of what was going on around me to let a lifetime of hopes and dreams suddenly slip away like that. This is an abridged version of the more detailed story I tell about my journey through sexual addiction in my first book, *Porn Nation: Conquering America's #1 Addiction.*

BACK TO THE FUTURE

The development of my sexual attitudes, beliefs, and behaviors from the time I was a college student up until the present day has greatly influenced the choices I've made throughout my life, large and small. As a teen and twenty-something, I basically rebelled against what I thought was a sexually repressed, puritanical upbringing because I thought I knew it all, including what it meant to be a real man. I was convinced that Hugh Hefner had it right, that real men were sexually liberated conquerors and real women were sex starved and sensuous playthings whose main purpose in life was to give men sexual pleasure. So I indulged as much as I could. While some chose to remain abstinent during that season of life, and others would occasionally dip their toes in the pool of sexual exploration just to test the water, I was out there swimming laps in what felt like a race against time, convinced that my peers who weren't indulging were sticks-in-the-mud who were missing out on a good and harmless thing. In my later years, as I became wiser to the realities of love, sex, relationships, and even porn, I constantly found myself fighting battles in my mind and in my body against the lies I had told myself, lies that had created a considerable amount of inertia that was constantly pushing me in the opposite direction of where I wanted to go with my life. Even as my sexual attitudes and beliefs were slowly starting to change, certain sexual behaviors and habit patterns were slow to follow after decades of entrenched thinking and doing. These habitual patterns would take much more work and far longer to change than I ever imagined.

Because I bought into all things pornographic back in college, I paradoxically have found myself back on college campuses sharing my personal life story and the lessons I learned along the way with today's college students. Some might call it fate; others consider it a vocation or a calling. I like to think that when the consequences of my choices finally broke me and my self-will, that the God of the universe reached down and mercifully steered me back to the very place where I wildly and willfully veered off course. I know that in my recovery I've had to go back several times to that point of interruption in my emotional and psychological development to deal with some very real issues that sent me off course. I've learned by observing my redemptive journey and those of others that it's not unusual to see some of the most passionate people helping others in areas that represent the greatest personal struggles and obstacles that they themselves have faced.

Like consulting a frequent traveler who knows every bend and hill along the trail that he's spent his whole life walking, we can all benefit from others' experience and learn to recognize the signs that we might have missed the first time around. That's called wisdom, and it's a rare and valuable gift that is not easily found or kept. With wisdom we see the things we were once blind to, and feel the things we were once numb to. Hard lessons learned are often ignored, causing many to shy away from past experiences in the hopes of forgetting the pain and disappointment. Yet some of us have been drawn back to them, embracing these defining moments of our past in the hopes that others headed down that same path might heed our warnings. Like a lone sentry patiently waiting to shine a light or sound a warning to all who come our way, we do this because we realize we may be the only hope they have of passing safely by. The question that remains is whether they will heed our warning, or blindly continue on by as we once did, convinced that our intellect or education or cunning is enough to dictate a different outcome.

The truth is, we are all living in a culture today that increasingly caters to our senses with the aim of creating insatiable appetites for goods and services. It's consumerism of the highest order, driven by the producer's pursuit of profits and the consumer's desire for immediate gratification and novelty. In this world, pornography and all things pornographic are modern-day "eye candy" that beckons us to come hither and explore. It calls out to us, offering a deeper connection with our desires than many of us were allowed to imagine while growing up. For some of us who grew up with a penchant for porn, we made such pursuits part of our "Great Escape," a secret fantasy world where for a time we could numb the pain, the guilt and shame, the anxiety, even the boredom that crept uninvited into our daily lives. Too young to grasp or even care about the price such pursuits would exact from us in later years, we continued to slip out of sight on occasion to sip the elixir and taste the forbidden fruit.

By the time many of us left home for college or the world of work, we had moved from sips to gulps, with our appetites for pornography growing as we continued to feed it under the auspices of "sexual freedom." For a time, there was no more hiding. No more restraint. We were the adults now, and this was our adult playground. We reasoned that this cheap form of entertainment was justifiable and harmless. A small diversion from the grand plan we had laid out for our lives. And so we told ourselves and others:

"It's only porn. It's not like I'm hurting anyone."

"I'm an adult now. I have a right to look at the material if I want to."

"It's just sex. There's nothing wrong with sex, so what's the harm in looking at pictures of naked women (and men) or watching people having sex?"

"Everybody looks at porn. A lot of people I know are into it. The only ones who don't look at porn are the prudes and puritans. After all, this *is* the twenty-first century."

"There's nothing wrong with looking at porn. It's freedom of speech— we all have a right to look at it if we want to. And if you don't like it, then just don't look at it."

Like I said earlier, I've walked this walk before. This is where I strayed, where I left the sure and narrow path for a broader one and the promise of better times ahead. So now I've returned as a frequent visitor and lecturer at Porn University. And I find for the most part it all looks and feels very much the same. It's still a place where free-flowing sexuality is the norm. And where tolerance still serves to disguise a certain amount of self-gratification that every person on campus seems to feel entitled to just because they're in college. We embrace this once-in-a-lifetime experience as an opportunity to pursue hedonistic pleasures, believing we can likewise suspend the laws of consequence if just for a season. Because it's college and we just want to have fun.

But what happens when the party's over and it's time to clean up the mess? Will we say it was worth it? Or will we have some regrets, even serious regrets, because of what we now know but never saw or recognized back then? For those of us who've been there, what will we say to those whom we see following in our footsteps? Will we remain silent, or will we sound a warning? Will we just stand by and watch as they repeat our mistakes? Or can we do something to reach out to them and help them understand that even in Porn University, things aren't always quite as harmless as they might appear. And that the consequences of their actions are certain to follow, if not tomorrow or next week or next month then certainly in a year, or five years, or even ten years from now when the stakes are much greater than they are today.

So what does it take for any of us to begin understanding the truth about ourselves? You can always start by taking a good hard look in the mirror.

CHAPTER 2

AM I
A SEX ADDICT?

Look into a mirror. What do you see? When I looked into the mirror back in 1997, just a few months after I had confessed to my wife that I was having an affair, I saw what I thought was a pretty good picture. I was an above-average guy who had been a successful businessman and a loving husband and father to my two boys. Granted, I had just cheated on my wife. But while I knew I was wrong, I somehow felt like I deserved to have a little fun on the side after thirteen years of marriage. Apart from what I considered to be an isolated moment of weakness in my life, I still liked what I saw when I looked in the mirror.

And then I got a phone call from a close friend. He sounded somber and claimed he had something important to tell me. "I'm a sex addict, I've got a sexual addiction."

My immediate response was one of bewilderment at this awkward "too much information" moment. "What's a sexual addiction, and why are you telling *me*?"

"Well, I've been watching you lately and listening to you go on about how Patty and you have grown apart, and how she isn't enough for you anymore, and how Teresa is your soul mate and all. And I'm starting to wonder if you're not a sex addict too."

I was pretty ticked off at that accusation even though I tried not to show it over the phone. After all, this "friend" had just accused me of having . . . well, I didn't know what it was at the time, but it sounded like an STD or something.

"Thanks for your concern and all, but . . . "

Yet before I could graciously bow out of this one, my friend boldly interrupted both my response and my life as I once knew it.

"Wait, before you totally dismiss what I'm saying, let me just tell you some of the things I've done, starting back when I was a kid." As he began sharing with me stories about his own experiences with porn and sex and girls and growing up, it sounded like he was telling *my story*! I was totally blown away, and a few minutes into it I knew he had nailed me—the *real* me—with this sexual addiction thing. That was the first mirror that served as a wake-up call, the reflection of my life as seen through the shared story of another who was just like me.

The second mirror is something I used shortly after my life-altering conversation with my friend. It was one of the first things I found while searching for resources and information on sexual addiction that helped me get a better understanding of what I might be up against. It was an online sex survey used to help determine whether or not a person might really be a sex addict. The Sexual Addiction Screening Test, or SAST, was developed in part by Dr. Patrick Carnes, the same man who had written many of the books I was reading on the subject. Dr. Carnes was a psychologist and pioneer of sorts in the area of sexual addiction and his first book, *Out of the Shadows*, had been recommended to me more than any other book on the topic. It was the first book I read by someone who really understood what sexual addiction was all about.

The SAST was only meant to be an early screening diagnostic tool that counselors, therapists, and other medical professionals could use to help determine the degree of compulsivity and the extent of addictive sexual behaviors that a patient might be exhibiting. Since this test is a brief survey of twenty-five yes or no questions that a respondent can complete on their own via the Web, it seemed like the ideal sex survey to use in conjunction with my speaking events in order to give students a simple tool to help them assess their own level of risk from sexually compulsive and addictive behaviors. In essence, allowing them to hold up a mirror to see for themselves how their own sexual attitudes, beliefs, and behaviors were impacting their lives from a clinical perspective. I kept thinking that maybe this would have helped me had it been available when I was in college.

So in the spring of 2005, we started promoting our events by directing students to go to a Web site we created called www.mysexsurvey.com to take the SAST, promising to maintain confidentiality and anonymity. The response from students was and continues to be overwhelming! For this book, we've analyzed the survey response results from surveys taken in the spring semester of 2006 through the spring semester of 2008. During this time period, 28,798 people took our online SAST. Ninety-three percent or 26,782 of the respondents were currently enrolled college students at the time. The remainder was mostly faculty or staff. The next section of this book is an examination and discussion of the key findings from the students' responses to this unprecedented survey.

It should be pointed out that the SAST is a diagnostic tool on which data continues to be collected. As a result, the cut-off scores for risk categories may change somewhat over time depending on how people respond to the test. The results are simply meant to be guidelines and suggestions and in no way replace a comprehensive assessment from a trained professional. Individuals may feel they are exhibiting sexually compulsive or addictive behaviors regardless of their score, which is one of the many reasons people should never forego seeking professional help for their problematic sexual behaviors. The score received at the end of the test is simply an accumulation of the total number of "yes" responses a person has. That sum total then puts that person in one of three ranges for "at risk" sexual behaviors: low risk, at risk, or high risk.

LOW RISK — 0 to 8 "yes" answers means the person may or may not have a problem with sexually compulsive behavior. However, if a person's sexual behavior is causing him problems in his life, he is encouraged to confide in a trusted friend for support and personal accountability and consider seeking the help of a professional counselor or health care specialist with experience in this area who can conduct further assessment.

AT RISK — 9 to 18 "yes" answers means the person is "at risk" for his sexual behavior to interfere with significant areas of his life. If he is concerned about his sexual behavior and has noticed consequences as a result, he should confide in a trusted friend for accountability and seek out the help of a professional counselor or health care specialist with experience in this area who can conduct a further assessment.

HIGH RISK — 19+ "yes" answers means the person is in the highest risk group for his sexual behavior to interfere with and jeopardize important areas of his life (social, occupational, educational, etc.). It is essential that he share this in confidence with a trusted friend willing to keep this confidential yet hold him accountable for his actions. It is also strongly recommended that he discuss his compulsive and addictive sexual behaviors with a professional counselor or health care specialist experienced in this area of work to further assess the situation and assist him.

Before getting to the twenty-five core diagnostic questions on the SAST, we had the respondents answer eight demographic and profile-related questions in areas of additional interest to us, such as what college or university they attended, what year they were in school, and how old they were when they were first exposed to pornography. The following chapter contains the complete SAST exactly as it appears in our online sex survey, including the introduction but excluding the risk assessment at the end (which was just discussed and reprinted above). Also included are the drop-down menu choices (indented) that were offered in the first eight questions. The test and results can be viewed online at www.pornuniversitythebook.com as well.

When you read through the twenty-five core questions, it quickly becomes evident that while some questions deal with factors that are known to be strong indicators of sexual dysfunction developed later in life (e.g., question 1, "Were you sexually abused as a child or adolescent?"), others could almost be considered common to the human experience (e.g., question 16, "Do you hide some of your sexual behavior from others?"). Yet, taken in their sum total and viewed in the context of an individual's overall struggle with unwanted sexual behavior, the SAST can and often does act as a kind of "early warning system." Especially when put in the hands of a student who might be in the midst of exploring his or her sexual identity, the SAST can open one's eyes to those factors that increase one's risk of developing sexually compulsive and addictive behaviors later in life. For instance, sexual abuse or incest earlier in life remains a strong influencer in the establishment of a faulty belief system regarding one's sexual self-image. So individuals with a history of abuse who take this test can start to see a more complete picture of why, for instance, they may be struggling with sexual compulsivity or other intimacy issues in relationships.

The SAST isn't a turnkey diagnostic solution in and of itself, of course. But for us it has served as much more than just a marketing tool. It's enabled us to create a safe environment around our Porn Nation events that helps us facilitate open, honest conversations about who we are and where we struggle as sexual beings. As mentioned, the next chapter contains the complete SAST, taken by more than twenty-eight thousand students, staff, and faculty who make up our campus communities. The complete results of the survey, showing the cumulative responses and filtered by gender, are located in the appendix. In chapter 4 we'll begin to focus on the students' responses to get a clearer picture of who they say they are and what they *really* think about sex on campus as well as how their choices have affected the way they see themselves and act toward others in relationships.

CHAPTER 3

THE SEXUAL ADDICTION SCREENING TEST

elcome to the Sexual Addiction Screening Test (SAST). Developed by Dr. Patrick Carnes, it's one of several diagnostic tools commonly used to help determine to what degree a person's sexual behaviors might have become compulsive or addictive.

The average time it takes to complete this 33 question survey is 5 minutes. Your individual responses will remain anonymous and strictly confidential. Data from this survey will be reported only in the aggregate.

When answering the 25 numbered yes/no questions, keep a running total of the number of your "yes" responses. At the end of the test, you'll find a general assessment of what your score might mean with regards to your overall sexual health. This test is in no way meant to be final or conclusive; it is just an early diagnostic tool.

Thank you for taking the time to complete this survey. To begin, click on the Continue button below.

1. Which college do you attend? (If your school isn't listed, check "Other" and specify)
   [Schools on the speaking tour for the current semester are listed]
   Other (please specify)_____

2. What is your gender?
   - ○ Male
   - ○ Female

3. Year in school or occupation?
   - ○ Freshman
   - ○ Sophomore
   - ○ Junior
   - ○ Senior
   - ○ Postgraduate
   - ○ Faculty
   - ○ Staff / Administration
   - ○ Other (specify)_____

4. What is your age?
   - ○ 18–21
   - ○ 22–25
   - ○ Over 25
   - ○ Under 18

5. Approximately how old were you when you first viewed pornography (sexually explicit material)?

○ 5 yrs. or younger	○ 9	○ 13
○ 6	○ 10	○ 14
○ 7	○ 11	○ 15
○ 8	○ 12	○ 16 yrs. or older

6. What form of pornography were you exposed to that first time?
   - ○ Internet or computer-based (photos or video)
   - ○ Soft or hard-core print magazines
   - ○ Soft or hard-core VHS or DVD movies
   - ○ Cable TV or pay-per-view
   - ○ Other (specify)_____

7. How many hours do you spend online per week?

○ Less than 5

○ 5–20

○ 21–50

○ Over 50

8. How many hours do you spend online for Internet sex per week?

○ 0

○ Less than 5

○ 5–20

○ Over 20

The next 25 "yes/no" questions make up the core Sexual Addiction Screening Test. All responses will be held in complete confidentiality and will only be used in aggregate with other survey respondents. Be sure to keep a running tally of how many questions you answer "yes" to. An explanation of what your score means immediately follows this test. Good luck!

1.	Were you sexually abused as a child or adolescent?	○ Yes	○ No
2.	Do you regularly read romance novels or sexually explicit magazines, or regularly visit sexually explicit web sites or chat rooms?	○ Yes	○ No
3.	Have you stayed in romantic relationships after they become emotionally or physically abusive?	○ Yes	○ No
4.	Do you often find yourself preoccupied with sexual thoughts or romantic daydreams?	○ Yes	○ No
5.	Do you feel that your sexual behavior is not normal?	○ Yes	○ No
6.	Does your spouse (or significant other(s)) ever worry or complain about your sexual behavior?	○ Yes	○ No

7. Do you have trouble stopping your sexual behavior when you know it is inappropriate? ○ Yes ○ No

8. Do you ever feel bad about your sexual behavior? ○ Yes ○ No

9. Has your sexual behavior ever created problems for you and your family or friends? ○ Yes ○ No

10. Have you ever sought help for sexual behavior you did not like? ○ Yes ○ No

11. Have you ever worried about people finding out about your sexual activities? ○ Yes ○ No

12. Has anyone been hurt emotionally because of your sexual behavior? ○ Yes ○ No

13. Have you ever participated in sexual activity in exchange for money or gifts? ○ Yes ○ No

14. Do you have times when you act out sexually followed by periods of celibacy (no sex at all)? ○ Yes ○ No

15. Have you made efforts to quit a type of sexual activity and failed? ○ Yes ○ No

16. Do you hide some of your sexual behavior from others? ○ Yes ○ No

17. Do you find yourself having multiple romantic relationships at the same time? ○ Yes ○ No

18. Have you ever felt degraded by your sexual behavior? ○ Yes ○ No

19. Has sex or romantic fantasies been a way for you to escape your problems? ○ Yes ○ No

20.	When you have sex, do you feel depressed afterwards?	○ Yes	○ No
21.	Do you regularly engage in sadomasochistic behavior (S&M, i.e., sex with whips, leather, spanking, pain, etc.)?	○ Yes	○ No
22.	Has your sexual activity interfered with your family life?	○ Yes	○ No
23.	Have you been sexual with minors?	○ Yes	○ No
24.	Do you feel controlled by your sexual desire or fantasies of romance?	○ Yes	○ No
25.	Do you ever think your sexual desire is stronger than you are?	○ Yes	○ No

Congratulations! You've just completed the SAST. Now make sure you go back and count the number of "yes" responses you had before continuing on to the Risk Assessment page [see p. 38 for Risk Assessment]. There you'll be able to find out what your score means and see how you did compared to others at your school and to peers on campuses throughout the world.

PART TWO

AND THE SURVEY SAID...

CHAPTER 4

A QUICK LOOK AT
DEMOGRAPHICS

While encouraging as many students as possible to take the SAST, we also wanted to collect a certain amount of demographic data for analysis so we knew who we were really talking to—or better yet, who was talking to us. There were also some nondemographic questions related to our study that we were curious about but that weren't a part of the SAST. So we asked eight questions that preceded the core twenty-five SAST questions (as shown in the last chapter). As with many aspects of our study analysis, our findings were interesting and sometimes unexpected.

The first four questions on the survey related to school affiliation, gender, year in school or occupation, and age. Because we only publicized the online survey site at the campuses where I was scheduled to speak, the majority of the respondents were students who attended those schools. However, as is often the case in our networked and interconnected culture, word spread and students attending over one thousand colleges and universities throughout the U.S. and Canada (and a few other countries)

47

ended up taking the survey.

In this book, we've included just the student responses in our final results analysis, and our purpose will be to study the overall trends rather than to report on specific details. If you are interested in a more detailed analysis of the results from specific schools and how their responses compared to other schools and the national averages, visit the Sex Survey page at www.pornuniversitythebook.com.

SCHOOL DEMOGRAPHICS

Each semester, we listed the names of those colleges and universities where I was scheduled to speak, as well as other large schools in the area, in a drop-down box on the survey's first question. Then, as a catchall for students who happened upon the survey through word of mouth or Internet social networking sites, we included an "other" category where they could write in the name of their school.

Although we only listed 110 colleges and universities over this three-year period of time (2006–2008), the respondents named more than 1,000 other schools from throughout the world as part of our "other" category. Of the 110 named schools, nearly half had over 100 student responses; 17 schools had over 500 student responses; and five schools had over 1,000. Those top five schools were the University of Wisconsin-Madison, 2,229; Purdue University (West Lafayette), 2,094; Indiana University (Bloomington), 1,219; University of California at Davis, 1,050; and the University of Southern California, 1,010.

In most cases, the number of students who took the online SAST was greater than the number of attendees at the actual presentation (for instance, approximately 1,100 students attended my talk at Indiana University while 1,219 took the SAST; 1,875 attended at Purdue while 2,094 took the test; and 1,450 attended at the University of Wisconsin-Madison but a whopping 2,229 took the SAST). However, on several campuses, there was little or no response to the SAST at all, typically because the local sponsors chose for whatever reason not to advertise it as part of the overall event. And as I mentioned earlier, students representing hundreds of campuses where we never held a Porn Nation event took the online test as well, most likely finding out about it from friends or through event ads placed by the sponsors on popular social networking sites like Facebook.

These results show that there is no direct relationship between taking the test and attending the event. We always encouraged the sponsors to promote the online sex survey (another name we used for the SAST) both before and after the event and encouraged the students on their campus to take the test, but it was never mandatory. When I would ask my audiences for a show of hands indicating how many had actually taken the online sex survey, the response varied widely, from less than 10% to over half of the students in attendance. Based on historical response rates though, we know that most of the tests are taken *before* my live speaking event, so that what I share and how I present the subject matter during my presentation seems to have little bearing on the results. We leave the site up indefinitely, so while the drop-down list of schools might change from semester to semester, students are free to take the test at any time.

It's also important to note that the posters and flyers that were typically used to promote Porn Nation events had a very porn-neutral message (neither pro nor con). Thus, it is unlikely that only a certain segment of the student population (mostly pro-porn or mostly anti-porn) would have responded to the advertising and taken the SAST to the exclusion of another group. In addition, the questions posed in the SAST, while very personal in nature, are also very objective (i.e., you either do or don't try to hide your sexual behavior from others; you either were or weren't sexually abused as an adolescent; etc.). So while there's always the chance that a student could take the test and lie in some or all of their responses, there is little incentive for them to do so. We also believe that due to the large number of students who took the test, the margin for error involved in discounting the responses of those who were dishonest or unknowingly untruthful is negligible in contrast to the overall trends and findings.

GENDER, CLASS, AND AGE DEMOGRAPHICS

Of the 28,798 respondents, 59% were male and 41% were female. The class breakdown was:

- Freshmen, 28%
- Sophomores, 21%
- Juniors, 19%
- Seniors, 17%
- Postgraduate, 8%.

The remaining 7% was a mix of faculty (1%), administrative staff (2%), and others (4%), but their responses are not included in the percentages we're reporting on throughout the rest of the book. Therefore, while currently enrolled college students made up 93% of the overall survey respondents, they represent 100% of our test question percentages that follow. Again, detailed breakdowns and cross-references of all the collected data are accessible by visiting our Web site, www.pornuniversitythebook.com.

In looking at the age demographic, as we expected, the 18- to 21-year-old traditional student age bracket made up the largest group of respondents at 70%, followed by ages 22–25 at 19%, over 25 at 10%, and under 18 at only 1%. Like everything else in college life, the younger the students, the more likely they are to get involved, including participating in surveys like this. I've found the same to be true of the demographics of those who typically attend my "Porn Nation" speaking events. Younger students always turn out in force.

But we were a little surprised that men made up a larger percentage of the survey respondents than women. Typically, I find that college women slightly outnumber the college men who attend my events. Many of the guys I talk to on campus are still pretty hesitant to talk openly about their sexuality, at least publicly and in a serious, self-examining way. Women, on the other hand, are typically eager to discuss all aspects of the subject matter, and a lot of them are seen dragging their boyfriends to the event.

One possible reason for the larger number of responses to this survey by males is the ability to take the online SAST in the privacy of your dorm room, house, or apartment. Maybe it's also because guys just seem to have a finely tuned sensor whenever the subject of sex is raised. Overall, even though we clearly explained in our pretest instructions that this was a clinically based screening test for sexual addiction, that didn't appear to dissuade a large number of students from taking the test, both males and females. I hope that's a good sign that today's college students are indeed interested in establishing or maintaining good sexual health and healthy relationships. At the very least it shows that they're still ever curious about the subject matter. But as the remainder of our survey responses show, that sexual curiosity manifests itself very differently today for young men than it does for young women.

CHAPTER 5

FIRST EXPOSURE:

MEN ARE FROM MARS, AND...

The next four preliminary questions on our survey (prior to the core twenty-five questions that make up the SAST) focus on exposure to pornography. We were especially interested in knowing just how much time our respondents spend using pornography in its most addictive form, Internet porn—what I and many experts in the area of addiction research refer to as the "crack cocaine" of sexual addiction.

In the early planning stages of this kind of study, I found that you bring with you certain assumptions and expectations about the results. Since I was first exposed to pornography at about age eleven, and since there has been a statistic floating around for years now that claims the average age of first exposure is eleven years old (a statistic, I might add, that appears largely unsubstantiated), I expected to see a similar average emerge from the data. If anything, I reasoned that cable TV, DVDs, and the dawning of the Internet age would have almost certainly driven that average age downward.

Furthermore, I didn't expect any substantial differences in the average age of first exposure for boys compared with girls. After all, those technologies and the pornographic material they have made so readily available are equal opportunity influencers. It just made sense that girls would be exposed to porn at just as early an age as boys, especially if their first exposure was "accidental," like in the process of doing homework online or flipping through TV channels. And all of the past "studies" seem to agree. However, in our survey results, a very different picture took shape. As far as the differences these students reported regarding their early exposure to and continued use of porn, it certainly makes you wonder, as the book by the same name suggests, if men really are from Mars and women from Venus.

"I'm addicted to porn ... please help."

~ COMMENT FROM A MALE
HIGH SCHOOL STUDENT

(Note to reader: unless stated otherwise, all comments are taken from feedback cards submitted by students and others attending a Porn Nation speaking event.)

AGE OF FIRST EXPOSURE

The first question in this group was straightforward: "Approximately how old were you when you first viewed pornography (sexually explicit material)?" The response options started at "5 years or younger" and increased in one year increments until "16 years or older." My assumption was that 100% of today's college students had been exposed to porn, and that most of them got their first look well under the age of 16. While the former may be true, I misjudged at what age the bulk of first exposures would occur, particularly as far as the women were concerned. It was here that I first noticed the disparity between men's and women's responses, a pattern that would repeat itself sporadically throughout our survey analysis.

The data showed that an even mix of men and women had their first exposure at 5 years and younger, 6 years old, even 7 years old. In fact, the percentages differed by only one point for each year up to age 9. But then, we noticed a separation started to occur. Take a look at the results:

What is most striking to me about these statistics is that they bust several myths that I think many people have about kids and their first exposure to porn. These responses suggest that the majority of boys are being exposed to porn at a much earlier age than the majority of girls. A total of 69% of all boys experienced first exposure between the ages of 10 and 14 while 68% of all girls faced first exposure from ages 13 and up, and over one-

AGE OF FIRST EXPOSURE	MEN	WOMEN
Up to 5 yrs.	2%	2%
6	1%	1%
7	2%	2%
8	4%	3%
9	4%	3%
10	10%	6%
11	9%	5%
12	19%	10%
13	18%	10%
14	13%	10%
15	8%	9%
16 yrs. and up	10%	39%

third of those girls, or 39%, never saw porn until after their 16th birthday. Put another way, 8 out of 10 boys (81%) were exposed to porn before they left the 8th grade compared to only half (52%) of the girls.

These spreads may not seem like much, especially since other studies have shown that nearly *every* college student today has had multiple exposures to hard-core porn long before stepping foot on campus. But what's eye-opening to me is that such a large group of boys are getting such a jump on the girls in viewing adult material. It really makes one wonder how much of that is accidental exposure versus an intentional searching out of the material. One also wonders how much of an influence our increasingly pornographic mainstream media—movies, music, cable TV, and video game plots and characters—are acting as enticements for younger children to proactively seek out more explicit pornographic material.

FORMS OF FIRST EXPOSURE

The next question looked at the sources of pornography, asking "What form of pornography were you exposed to the first time?" Again, boys and girls were similar in some respects and very different in others. Predictably, yet alarmingly, Internet or computer-based photos or videos played a significant role in giving kids their first taste of porn—interestingly, affecting the same number of girls as boys at roughly one-third or 35%.

Surprisingly, though, the Internet wasn't as significant a medium for boys as it was for girls. In fact, 39% of all boys were first exposed to porn through hard- or soft-core magazines. Like father, like son I suppose, since adult magazines have been the primary gateway to other forms of pornography for men for decades. After the Internet and computer-based porn, girls mentioned cable TV or pay-per-view as the second most common medium for first exposure, followed by soft- or hard-core magazines and soft- or hard-core VHS or DVD movies. The guys followed up their second choice, the Internet, with cable TV or pay-per-view and soft- or hard-core VHS or DVD movies last.

> *"I actually struggled with addiction to pornography at a really young age ... and I am a female. I was introduced to porn when I was seven years old and had a real addiction until sixteen years old."*

FORM OF FIRST EXPOSURE	MEN	WOMEN
Internet or computer-based (photos or video)	35%	35%
Soft- or hard-core print magazines	39%	20%
Soft- or hard-core VHS or DVD movies	10%	18%
Cable TV or pay-per-view	13%	24%
Other	2%	3%

So magazines and the Internet rule the day for the guys while the girls find the Internet and cable TV or pay-per-view to be their culprits. Content providers, it should be duly noted, are supposed to make clear indications whenever the content is intended for mature or adult audiences only. It should also be noted that these warnings, whether on Internet porn sites or as the lead-in to a TV program or rented movie, have never been much of a deterrent to consumption by adolescents and teens. If anything, they send a signal to underage consumers that says, "Here it is! Just what you've been looking for! The edgy stuff." Parents, of course, should make use of these caveats in order to screen what their kids will be exposed to.

YOUNG ADULTS AND ADULT MATERIAL

So what happens when kids do grow up to become adults? How much time do young adults in college spend looking at "adult material" or pornography? Answering this question is a study in itself, and while it wasn't our main focus, we were curious to learn how much time college students would say they were spending online for Internet sex per week—looking at porn, hanging out in sex-related chat rooms, soliciting others for sex, etc.

First, however, we needed to know how much time they were spending online overall to arrive at a baseline for comparison. So we began with, "How many hours do you spend online per week?" Indeed, with coursework, grades, and research material now accessible online, not to mention the ubiquitous social networking phenomenon, it's hard if not impossible to survive in college these days without being connected to the Web. We discovered that the majority of both genders were very similar in the amount of time they were spending on the Internet, with the largest percentage of each spending 5 to 20 hours per week online. Here's the breakdown:

So just how much time is being spent by students taking a detour from the alternating stress and boredom of college life to peruse porn? We asked those same stu-

HOURS SPENT ONLINE / WEEK	MEN	WOMEN
Less than 5 hours	10%	11%
5–20 hours	52%	57%
21–50 hours	30%	27%
50+ hours	8%	6%

dents, "How many hours do you spend online for Internet sex per week?"

I realize the wording of this question could have left some students scratching their heads, wondering exactly what qualifies as "Internet sex."

> *"I could relate... because my dad cheated on my mother and watching all these images from a young age put 'this is good' in my mind and I had an eating disorder for six years."*
>
> ~ COMMENT FROM A
> FEMALE COLLEGE STUDENT

In this case, I purposefully left it ambiguous and open to the interpretation of each respondent. What was more important to me than giving a narrow definition of the term was that the respondents used their own interpretation of whether or not they were engaged in sex over the Internet. In other words, I trusted their judgment and willingness to answer honestly and to the best of their knowledge. The last thing I wanted was for a student to bail out on the test midstream (although some did anyway) because they disagreed with what we asked or how we asked it. If *they* thought it was for sex, that's what really mattered—that and their truthful responses.

In one of the most revealing results of this entire study, the responses to this final demographic question show that when it comes to pursuing sex on the Internet, college women and college men could hardly be further apart. For starters, the overwhelming majority of college women aren't even interested in Internet sex, whether that means viewing porn, participating in sex chat rooms, using web cams for sexual exposure, or looking for a hookup for the night.

> *"Most of the guys I know are really into porn."*
>
> ~ COMMENT FROM A
> FEMALE COLLEGE STUDENT

In fact, 82% of the college women we surveyed say they spend 0 hours per week online for Internet sex, while only 36% of the guys gave the same answer. In this case, I do wish I had stipulated that having Internet sex includes viewing pornography and having sex with yourself (masturbation). Most guys are legendary liars when it comes to talking about masturbation, including whether or not they would consider masturbating to Internet porn a form of sex. Yet even with that in mind, 51% of the guys admitted to spending up to 5 hours per week online for Internet sex compared to a measly 16% of all college women. Furthermore, only 2% of college women said they spent more than 5 hours per week online for sex, but a whopping 11% of guys spend 5–20 hours and another 2% spend *over* 20 hours per week pursuing sex on the Web—six times as many men as women.

HOURS SPENT ONLINE / WEEK FOR INTERNET SEX	MEN	WOMEN
0 hours	36%	82%
Less than 5 hours	51%	16%
5–20 hours	11%	1%
Over 20 hours	2%	1%

PORNOGRAPHY: SEX ED FOR GUYS

Demographic and profiling questions aren't usually all that interesting when it comes to studies like these. But in the case of our series of questions leading up to the core SAST, we were able to see a clearer picture of just when and how today's college students began their lifelong relationship with pornography and cybersex.

The majority of the men who took our survey were first exposed to porn long before they entered high school, typically around the age of puberty or shortly thereafter. A third of them were first exposed via the most toxic form, Internet porn. I say "toxic" because you're always just a few clicks away from sampling images and video depicting anything from the mildest nude images to the most obscene "money shots" ranging from fetishes and bestiality to rape scenes and child pornography. Scenes and images the mind is not likely to soon forget, if ever. And while we didn't ask about their continued use of the material throughout adolescence and during high school, we were able to capture a snapshot of the average college male and their level of involvement with porn and sex on the Internet.

> *"Masturbation is healthy. Porn can be empowering. Open sexual dialogue is important, masturbation and pornography are not victimless crimes, they are victimless pastimes."*
> ~ COMMENT FROM A MALE COLLEGE STUDENT

59

What we see is that nearly two-thirds of all college men are still pursuing a relationship with porn and cybersex in varying degrees of frequency and intensity. No wonder it's common to hear college women these days saying, "All of the guys in college look at porn."

As for college women, most weren't exposed to pornography until later on in their teenage years, and at least a third were exposed after they turned 16. And while it's a fact that more and more women are reporting that they struggle with their thought life because of their early exposure to the material, far more have a "take it or leave it . . . if that's what they want to look at" attitude toward the material and the guys they know who are into porn. But as for themselves, in spite of the best efforts of an adult entertainment industry determined to grow by producing more material that's specifically geared toward a largely untapped female audience, the overwhelming majority of college women (82%) at least have decided they can live without it and simply ignore that porn even exists. Their primary sex education is coming from other sources, including our sex-saturated mainstream media.

"Porn fosters healthy adult relationships. . . . I have lots of sex, and I have serious friends. . . . Sex is a normal part of human existence, no matter what way you treat it. . . . It was worship of the orgasmic experience."
~ COMMENT FROM A MALE COLLEGE STUDENT

But as we're about to see as we start examining the responses of both sexes to the SAST's core questions, and in spite of their divergent appetites for the empty calories that pornography represents, there is much more going on beneath the surface than might appear. We have found that many of our next generation leaders already bear the scars of this subtle form of sexual abuse. And yet, we also see promising signs that if there is any generation that is capable of seeing through the false intimacy and the tacky veneer of our increasingly pornographic society, this one can.

CHAPTER 6

STUDENTS
BEHAVING BADLY:
PORN U'S
WALKING WOUNDED

efore the age of the Internet and the proliferation of Internet porn, sexual addiction was a strange and controversial malady that few understood—and many people even questioned its legitimacy. Dr. Patrick Carnes, a pioneer in this field of study, pointed out the high incidence of sexual addiction among people who were victims of sexual abuse, incest, and other sexual trauma early in their childhood. Many of those same men and women would go on to sexually abuse themselves and others, including spouses and children.

While exposure to and use of pornography seemed to play a role in most of these cases, especially by the abuser, it was not uncommon for a survivor of sexual abuse to become sexually addicted later in life without being a regular consumer of pornography. Other far more damaging behaviors had typically taken root by then, with pornography having long since been bypassed as a rather mild stimulant to the neurotransmitters in the pleasure/pain pathways of the brain. In other words, they had become numb and desensitized to the material long ago.

That's just a brief snapshot of the complex and often tortured existence of a sexual abuse survivor. Although sexual abuse is not a prerequisite for developing a sexual addiction later in life, it is still a strong predictor. For that reason, there are several questions scattered throughout the SAST that ask point-blank about the respondent's history both as a victim of sexual abuse and as an abuser. In this chapter, we'll visit those questions and the students' responses to see what they might mean for the rest of us.

Because those affected by sexual abuse are Porn U's "walking wounded," it's important that we take great care in discussing their plight, especially during these critical young adult years in college. But it's also just as important to remind them that their past, whether as abuser or the abused, doesn't have to be the prologue to the rest of their lives. Today there are more resources than ever to give real hope and help to survivors of sexual abuse. We also have a far greater understanding today of how the brain— our largest and most powerful sex organ—processes and responds to sexual stimuli, both properly and pathologically. That's not only key in knowing how to get the right kind of help to those who are hurting the most, but it's also important in helping us better understand how they got that way in the first place, especially as we start to deal with an increasing number of people who are the victims of a new kind of self-abuse brought on by their voluntary consumption of pornography.

SEXUAL ABUSE

The first question in the SAST gets right to the heart of the matter: "Were you sexually abused as a child or adolescent?"

The responses from the students were very much in line with what we now know about the incidence of sexual abuse in our society. Specifically, 5% of the college men answered "yes" while more than twice as many college women (12%) admitted that they were sexually abused earlier in life.

It can't be emphasized enough just how important this statistic is. Initial childhood and adolescent sexual experiences, whether through early exposure to pornography or being sexually abused by others, have a way of leaving a permanent impression on more than just a person's mind or memory. They traumatize our very souls and injure our spirits, convincing many to think of themselves as "damaged goods."

These beliefs are common in the abuse victim's no-win world of self-hatred and self-condemnation. No matter how mild or how strong those feelings might be, they often form the very foundation of a faulty belief system common to all sexual addicts. Whether it's believing that sex equals love (as in the case of incest where a parent tells a child that by having sex with them, the parent is simply expressing their love for them), or believing that no one would love them if they knew everything about them (as in the secrets a sexually abused child is often forced to keep), abuse victims are especially susceptible to a number of "false truths" that then become the basis of their faulty belief system. Without help, these individuals face a lifetime of struggles with self-esteem, self-image, and body image issues as well as having difficulty building trust or maintaining healthy intimate relationships with others.

> *"Thank you for saying, 'If I tell people who I am, no one will love me.' I was raped at age five and eight and continually molested til age fourteen and your words (esp. coming from a man) have added to my healing process. You made me cry (that's good)."*
>
> ~ COMMENT FROM A FEMALE COLLEGE STUDENT

Consider the words of this female college student I met several years ago at one of my Porn Nation events who shared her story with me in an email:

I was raped in the 8th grade, and ever since that I always thought that guys only wanted one thing, and I gave it to them freely. That's how I was trying to fill the emptiness I had inside of me, to have a quick feeling of love. I would have 5 guys in my life at one time. I would sleep with each of

*them and then decide how they can benefit me. The one that gave me good
sex, I would use him for booty call. The one good with foreplay, that's all
he was used for, etc. I looked at guys as sex toys, someone to please me.
And I always had to be in charge. When people say porn, I would think of
a dirty old man. I never thought of myself like that. But after hearing you
speak, I realized I am porn.*

With women dominating this sex abuse statistic in our survey's results by more than a 2 to1 margin over the men, it should come as no surprise that our survey also shows more than twice as many college women as men have admitted to staying in romantic relationships after their partners have become emotionally or physically abusive—23% of the women versus 10% of the men. That's 1 out of every 4 women on campus compared to only 1 in 10 men—a sad but true testament to the fact that women (and men) who are sexually abused early in life constantly battle the collateral damage of abuse manifested in strained relationships with others and unhealthy images of themselves.

> "*I have dealt with sexual abuse in the past, and hearing Michael's epiphany made me sort of relive these issues and revisit my self-degradation for a man who abused me and left me for the more promiscuous girl.*"
>
> ~ COMMENT FROM AN OLDER FEMALE STUDENT

The woman who shared her story with me in the email above went on to describe how her sexually abusive past had impacted her relationships:

> "*The last 'relationship' I was in, the guy was cheating on his girlfriend with me. When I found out, it hurt because I thought I was the only one. But yet I still wanted to be with him.*"

Sexual abuse does significant damage to survivors and society as a whole, and the normalization of this kind of abuse played out in pornography is only making the related problems more prevalent.

HARMFUL SEXUAL BEHAVIORS

Another indicator of this tendency of abuse victims to self-abuse and even abuse others surfaced in this question's results: "Do you regularly engage in sadomasochistic behavior (S&M, i.e., sex with whips, leather, spanking, pain, etc.)?"

This question appears on the Sexual Addiction Screening Test because regardless of the defense those who participate in such sexual behaviors put up to try to legitimize their actions, psychologists know all too well that combining sex with pain is pathological and unhealthy and often points to other problem areas rooted in an individual's past. Once again, while the overall percentages were small, women outpaced the men by nearly 2 to 1 (8% vs. 5%) in admitting that they regularly pursue sexual pleasure by experiencing and inflicting physical and sexual pain.

While our survey revealed that girls and young women are being sexually victimized at a higher rate than boys and young men, it also showed indications that men were much more likely to be the abusers than women.

The question was, "Have you ever been sexual with minors?" While only 5% of all college women admitted they had been sexual with a minor, almost three times as many men, or 13%, said they were guilty of this serious offense. Since it's a crime in every state for an adult to have sex with a minor, this is not an insignificant statistic. Essentially, it says that 1 in 10 college males are criminally guilty of having sexually violated a minor as an adult.

Combine that legacy with the fact that a large majority of college males have been regular consumers of pornography since before puberty, and typically at an earlier age than girls, and it's not hard to understand why so many more men than women have faulty sexual belief systems and thus show an early history of out-of-bounds sexual behavior. Although one certainly doesn't have to be a sex addict in order to cross the line from acceptable to unacceptable sociosexual behavior, young fans of porn put themselves at greater risk. And if you don't believe me, I have a stack of letters from men who are sitting in prison because of their affinity for porn that began at an early age and continued to grow until they acted out sexually. As I often stressed in my first book, the fact is, "What you feed grows, and what you starve dies."

PAYING FOR SEX

Another question regarding out-of-bounds sexual behavior that we asked was, "Have you ever participated in sexual activity in exchange for money or gifts?"

In yet another indicator of this greater tendency of males than females to develop harmful sexual pathologies, 1 in 10 guys responded "yes" versus only 1 in 20 women. As I travel across the country, I hear plenty of stories of strippers being hired to perform at parties held in frat houses and in off-campus housing. Porn parties are also popular today, where the suds flow freely and porn is the focal point of the night's entertainment. Whether it's porn videos playing on the big screen in the background or sex acts being staged involving two or more people (usually with hired strippers or professional porn actors and actresses), porn-themed parties are becoming more frequent occurrences on campus. Coincidentally, pictures and videos of college porn parties make up one of the fastest growing and most popular genres of the porn industry, often referred to as "gonzo" or reality porn. It's also helped give birth to the "new pornographers," amateur videographers and photographers who are very often students themselves. As they post their materials online, whether for the private viewing of friends or for public exposure to all who visit, they are literally changing the face of the porn industry as we know it.

While it's not unusual to hear about college women being in the audience at these porn parties and stripper extravaganzas, the most common reaction I get from the women on campus when asked about the guys' penchant for porn is usually a sly grin or a smirk and shrug of the shoulders, followed by nonchalant replies like, "Yeah, a lot of guys I know are into strippers and porn." Most college women are aware that this is going on, but very few seem concerned and fewer still seem to take it seriously. Perhaps this is understandable, since many of these same women stopped taking porn seriously themselves not long after they were first exposed as older teens. They represent a vast segment of the population whom pornographers salivate over but have repeatedly failed to entice and convert into active porn consumers. To many college women, pornography and the pornographic, hypersexual attitudes and behaviors many guys exhibit on campus represent silly, boyish antics that most mistakenly consider to be harmless fun. Since many of them quickly abandoned their early fascination with porn, the majority of college women I've spoken with tend to assume that most guys will eventually abandon it as well, especially when offered real sex as an alternative.

But what most of today's college women don't understand is that it's unlikely many of their male counterparts will ever cease to have some kind of a relationship with pornography, especially those who have become such avid consumers by the time they're in college. As this large group of guys and smaller group of women continue to feed these sexual images and messages to their brain, many will become desensitized and crave ever more graphic forms of porn to achieve the same level of dopamine production and thus sexual stimulation. In the process, statistics show that about 6–8% of them will find that compulsive masturbation to pornography has become an addictive behavior they can't live without, especially in times of stress and conflict.

CONCLUSIONS

The sexual abuse and pathologies focused on in this chapter from the SAST responses highlight some of the leading indicators of compulsive and addictive sexual behaviors. Anyone answering "yes" to any of these questions is throwing up a huge red flag over his head that should read "Help Me!" However, as those of us familiar with sexual addiction and recovery know all too well, the tendency of these "walking wounded" is to hide in guilt and shame from the very people who can help the most. It's something we've done all of our lives. We've built a fantasy world out of porn and sexual acting out behaviors that has become our "Great Escape" from the stresses and boredom and pain of everyday life. It's a secret world we've created, and in it we hide. When others get close to discovering our secrets, we lie. We fabricate a new reality for ourselves out of the expectations that others have for us and wear it around like a mask, taking it off and putting it on whenever necessary. It's a game we play because we feel we need to in order to survive — because beneath our chameleon-like defenses, we know we are guarding deep wells of guilt and shame that we dare not let anyone else see. Guilt, shame, hurt, and pain represent our greatest fears, so we defend our long-held secrets.

Those "walking wounded" among us feel very much like this. I know because I spent most of my life standing guard over my secret world and I used sex and porn as a way to try to maintain my equilibrium. However, I was different from those we've been talking about in this chapter. I was not the victim of sexual abuse as a child or adolescent nor was I ever in a sexually or physically abusive relationship; I never had sex with a minor as an adult; I've never been into S&M; and I never exchanged sex for money or gifts. Yet I had a thirty-year relationship with pornography that escalated over time into a sexual addiction and culminated in an affair with a female sex and relationship addict that cost me everything. Even my fairly normal childhood and family-of-origin issues played something of a role in putting me on a similar path to those we've spoken about in this chapter. The common ground we shared was a growing sense of guilt and shame in who we were and what we had become as sexual beings. Sexual attitudes and behaviors were born out of faulty beliefs we held about ourselves and others, and that's where all the trouble began.

The universal truth underlying all addictions and most mental illnesses is that faulty belief systems beget faulty lives and dysfunctional relationships. A longtime mantra among computer software programmers is "Garbage in, garbage out." That saying is all too true for those of us who've been operating much of our lives on a false set of assumptions and beliefs. After all, rocket scientists didn't get to where they are by *not* believing in the law of gravity. It represents absolute truth to them, so much so that everything they do takes this physical law into consideration.

Similar universal truths exist related to our physical, psychological, emotional, and even spiritual makeup as humans, including who and what we are as sexual beings. But it's what we believe about who we are that defines us. In these laws and principles that make up the description of who we are as sexual beings, we all pay a steep price for getting it wrong. We suffer the consequences and create a conflicted inner climate of fear, uncertainty, and doubt—the perfect breeding ground for what are widely considered the two most important factors that drive the addictive cycle: guilt and shame.

CHAPTER 7

SEX ON THE BRAIN

In the last chapter we examined the prevalence of sexual abuse and pathologies that many college students struggle with today. Now we want to take a closer look at how they responded to a broader set of questions relating to the use of sex and pornography in their everyday lives.

Unlike the questions and issues we examined in the last chapter, which pertain to a small but significant minority of college students, these responses encompass a far larger group—and at times a majority—of the students we surveyed. This next set of questions seeks to gain a clearer picture of what kind of relationship students have with sex and pornography—how they see it, and how they use it.

REGULARITY OF CONSUMPTION

The second question in the SAST expands on an earlier question from the demographics section that asked how many hours per week the respondent spent for Internet sex. This second question asked, "Do you regularly read romance novels or sexually explicit magazines, or regularly visit sexually explicit web sites or chat rooms?" (While romance novels are generally viewed in our culture and by most men as innocent, nonpornographic reading material, they're commonly cited by women who struggle with everything from unwanted sexual fantasies to love and relationship addiction as a "gateway drug" that started them down a path of later consuming more pornographic material or acting out sexually with others.)

> *"My roommate uses porn like 6 or 7 times a day."*
> ~ COMMENT FROM A MALE COLLEGE STUDENT

I expected that the percentages of "yes" responses to this question would equal or exceed the total percentage of students who indicated in our earlier question that they were spending any amount of time online for Internet sex. That was the case with the women—20% said "yes" to this question compared to 18% who answered that they spent some amount of time on the Internet for sex.

> *"I don't watch it alone. It's usually with my boyfriend."*
> ~ COMMENT FROM A FEMALE COLLEGE STUDENT

When it came to the guys, however, some of them must have either changed their minds in the span of only two questions, or more likely decided that their consumption of porn was infrequent enough to not be considered "regular." Maybe seeing the term "romance novels" placed first in the question threw them off. Or, of course, a number of them may have simply chosen to lie (that wouldn't be the first time a person lied on a survey about sex). It's also not uncommon for people who regularly view porn to minimize the actual amount of time they spend looking at the material.

> *"I kind of like porn. I own some porn. I'm a pretty big fan of it."*
> ~ COMMENT FROM A MALE COLLEGE STUDENT

Whatever the reason, only 42% of the men answered "yes" to this question, although 64% admitted earlier in the test to spending some amount of time every week online pursuing Internet sex. So whether it's 42% or 64% or somewhere in between, it's still much more time than their female counterparts are spending looking at porn.

THOUGHT LIFE

The next question we'll consider moved from asking about one's behavior to one's thought life: "Do you often find yourself preoccupied with sexual thoughts or romantic daydreams?"

It may surprise some to learn that the percentage of college women (62%) who often find themselves preoccupied with such thoughts isn't much different from the percentage of college men (68%). As to what exactly it is they're imagining, well, that may be a completely different story.

As I tour college campuses sharing my personal story from the stage with mixed audiences of both men and women, I usually get confused looks from the women whenever I start to describe how men tend to be "visual." I'll share about how I used to mentally undress some women I'd meet, trying to imagine what they looked like naked or what it might be like to have sex with them. Then I would have a stored mental image of the woman that I could recall over and over again, depending on how strong the attraction was. Sometimes I would revisit those thoughts and images several times that day, and again later that week, and even months or years later. Yes, years later! Before I ever discovered porn, I remember being fascinated by the X-ray glasses ads in the back of *Boys' Life* magazine and their promise of allowing me to see through other people's clothes. Later in life, pornography made that fantasy thought a reality for me. Because of these early adolescent experiences, I would never look at women or their clothing the same way again.

On the whole, I find that most women are appalled that a guy's mind could work that way. Even today, in a world where porn is the norm in our mainstream media and everything from clothing to chat room conversations have taken on a distinctly pornographic undertone, women who learn the truth about the hypersexed thought life of the majority of men are often stunned and amazed. And I'm equally stunned and amazed, as I'm sure most guys are, at how this seems to blindside them.

For Women Only by Shaunti Feldhahn is a groundbreaking book about what really goes on in the inner lives of men. This Harvard-educated author, who conducted extensive surveys and interviewed hundreds of men, came up with seven revelations about men that she claimed would be news to most women, as they were to her. In her chapter dealing with the true meaning of the statement "men are visual," the author writes, "Here's the insight I stumbled on by accident, which has radically reshaped my understanding of men: Even happily married men are instinctively pulled to visually 'consume' attractive women, and these images can be just as alluring whether they are alive or recollected."[1]

> *"I think [porn is] really gross personally. I don't think it's something that should be out in the open the way it is, especially on the Internet."*
>
> *"Sure, everyone looks at porn. Like at parties and stuff, people just kind of like randomly flash people and stuff, but that's not really porn."*
>
> ~ COMMENTS FROM TWO FEMALE COLLEGE STUDENTS

In a survey Feldhahn conducted of 800 men, 87% admitted that they have a mental set of sensual images that rise up or can be conjured up in their minds, something she describes as our "mental Rolodexes."[2] It's more like a fully automated mass storage system with gigabytes of high-speed memory if you ask me. Since only 25% of women describe themselves as being "visual,"[3] this characteristic so common among men is understandably a mystery to most women. For men or women who are more visually oriented, it's easy to see why pornography can be such a major influence in the formation of their sexual belief system.

But what about those who aren't as sexually aroused by visual images as they are by relational or emotional sexual fantasies ("Hmm, my first name sounds great with his last name. He's so great with his kids. I wonder what our kids would look like?")? This is a more common scenario for women who become sex addicts—often referred to as love and relationship addicts. While less driven by visual images, these women's beliefs and behaviors are no less compulsive and addictive than their visually driven male and female counterparts. For instance, I'm now quite certain that the woman I had an affair with was a love and relationship addict. A year after my divorce while still living in denial of the severity of my sexual addiction, I came to discover that she was also seeing and sleeping with at least five other married men with families. As I discovered the truth about her and saw how sick she was, I started to see the truth about me and how sick I was too. That was the breakthrough I needed to finally realize that I needed help in order to stop my sexually compulsive and addictive behaviors so I could start to get well.

RELATIONSHIPS

One of the questions in the SAST seeks to uncover such dysfunctional relationship tendencies as a potential contributing factor to problematic sexual behaviors. The question asks, "Do you find yourself having multiple romantic relationships at the same time?"

Interestingly, the response rate was nearly identical for both women and men—13% and 14%, respectively. While the overall number of men and women involved in multiple, simultaneous romantic relationships is low, those who develop a repeated pattern of such behavior (grouped together with several other high risk behaviors and attitudes cited in the SAST) show a characteristic common to most sex addicts—the need for new and novel forms of sexual arousal. For individuals with this kind of relationship history, having multiple partners and frequently switching relationships is typically regarded as a form of intimacy avoidance. As new relationships age, the heightened state of sexual arousal diminishes along with that person's interest in staying in the relationship.

> *"I am only 20 yrs old and have had at least 15 partners."*
>
> *"I had 60 dates in a 45 day period. It was just that desire, that need to feel loved, to feel wanted."*
>
> ~ COMMENTS FROM TWO FEMALE COLLEGE STUDENTS

SEXUAL FANTASIES

One telling question that the SAST poses regarding an issue that is almost always present in the case of sexually compulsive and addictive disorders (including love and relationship addiction) is, "Has sex or romantic fantasies been a way for you to escape your problems?"

Here, nearly a third of both groups—33% of the men and 29% of the women—said "yes." Once again, while this activity alone isn't enough to declare that one is or will likely become a sex addict one day, it is a nearly universal experience among those who are. In my first book, *Porn Nation*, I dedicated an entire chapter to this dynamic, which I titled "The Great Escape." Escapism through sexual fantasies and porn was a coping mechanism I started to develop in early adolescence that never really went away as I got older. The schemes just became more sophisticated and complex. Being discovered by others in the midst of my shameless private acts was never an option, either as a child or an adult. But the extra effort to hide my behaviors seemed worth it because of the reprieve from stress and worry I experienced by this momentary state of euphoria and arousal. It just felt too good to let go.

"I started using porn when I was in high school and have always struggled with sexual thoughts and fantasies. I've mentally raped hundreds and hundreds of guys long before I ever came to this campus. It's caused real problems for me in every relationship I've been in."

~ COMMENT FROM A FEMALE COLLEGE STUDENT

While sexually compulsive and addictive behaviors were still a long way off for me as an adolescent, the way I used the material to both pleasure myself and escape from reality set a bad precedent. That behavior, along with my father's habitual abuse of alcohol, and spending time with school friends who used pot, cocaine, and pharmaceuticals only exasperated my dependence on porn. In the overall food chain of all the different ways to escape, porn and sex hardly even registered on the "harmful" scale to most of my friends and me. But I used everything at my disposal to escape the feelings I didn't like: stress, conflict, anger, disappointment, insecurity, boredom, low self-esteem, embarrassment, and of course, shame and guilt. In my family growing up, where projecting a positive, upbeat image was always valued and rewarded far more than expressing negative emotions and creating conflict, there were plenty of opportunities to stuff my negative feelings.

Despite this, for the most part I grew up in a pretty stable environment. Mom and Dad seldom fought, never divorced, and there was always plenty of love to go around for the five of us kids. Each of us contributed our fair share of drama to our family life, myself at times more than the rest. Looking back, I wouldn't trade places with anyone or any other family. Yet there were times growing up when I felt just the opposite.

Discovering that nearly a third of today's college students use sex or romantic fantasies to escape the problems of everyday life concerns me. It concerns me because I know just how intoxicating that form of escapism can be. It concerns me because I also know how much more available my drug of choice is today to anyone who goes looking for it. And it concerns me because of how socially acceptable this method of escapism has become in all of its varied forms. In fact, across broad segments of our culture, it's almost expected and sometimes even applauded and celebrated as a hopeful sign to some of their long-awaited liberation from an allegedly stifling, puritanical, sexually starved society.

> *"There's nothing wrong with porn just like there's nothing wrong with sex. And those that think so are just stuck in an old, puritanistic, repressive mind-set."*
>
> ~ COMMENT FROM A MALE COLLEGE STUDENT

CONCLUSION

I hear a lot of talk on our college campuses about ridding the world of anything resembling our supposed Puritan-style sexual values. In some people's minds this is a battle we're already losing. When it comes to discussing sexually related topics like pornography, sexual addiction, and sexual abuse versus the amount of airtime we devote to pornography and sexual exploitation, maybe these are the dark ages. Still, if you visit today's universities and count the number of recognized student organizations dedicated to the cause of any of a wide variety of sexual orientations or genres, you would think that absolute sexual freedom already exists for all.

The official position throughout our academies of higher education and learning appears to be that when it comes to sex, anything and everything goes. That is, just as long as no one gets hurt. The lofty ideal is that anyone's chosen sexual identity or orientation deserves acceptance and tolerance by everyone else. In fact, the more unique, unusual, and extreme, all the more reason to spotlight and celebrate it. That environment would have been considered nirvana by many of us who pursued porn and grew up in the wake of America's sexual revolution of the '60s. A friend of mine who was also sexually active during his college years made this tongue-in-cheek observation about his and my unique relationship to America's sexual past and present: "We were born a few decades too soon." That would certainly seem to be the case as far as hedonists are concerned.

So what about it? What harm can there be in living a sex-centric life the way it's portrayed in the pages of *Playboy* and *Penthouse* or *Magnum* and *Cosmo* magazines? What's wrong with living according to a sexual belief system inspired by porn and our sex-saturated society, especially if we can figure out a way to manage it? You know, derive all of the benefits without experiencing any of the consequences. I see that reasoning at work in the eyes of some defiant students I talk to, students who are much like I once was. We reason that we're smart enough, educated enough, crafty and clever and strong-willed enough to play the game our way and win. We pretend not to see the lies and the real lives behind the printed and digital images we consume, dumbing down our feelings so we don't have to consider the feelings and fate of others.

But does it really work? Or are we fooling ourselves into thinking that we won't be affected in some way we may not fully understand? Can we really avoid the consequences of our Great Escape, or have we overestimated our ability to win on our terms without losing something far more valuable that lies undiscovered within us? Borrowing a favorite phrase from a well-known pop-culture psychologist, maybe we should spend more time asking the question of ourselves and one another, "So how's that working for you?"

CHAPTER 8

SO HOW'S THAT

WORKING FOR YOU?

All too often we discover our weaknesses and become self-aware much too late in the game. By then we've damaged ourselves and inflicted pain on others. As this reality sets in, so does the guilt and shame, and suddenly we find there's no one left to blame but ourselves.

In all of my research, interviews, and personal experiences regarding sexual addiction, an often-repeated theme is the central role that guilt and shame play in the addictive cycle. In a nutshell, it goes something like this: we "act out" an unwanted sexual behavior that instills guilt and shame in us. Because the resulting guilt and shame create inner conflict and negative feelings about ourselves, we start looking for a way to escape the pain. As our willpower weakens, we escape the pain by turning to our drug of choice (porn, relationships, and the like). But the relief is only temporary and usually comes at the expense of new consequences brought on by our acting out behavior (lost time, responsibilities ignored, etc.). As we return to reality and the problems of everyday life, we swear and promise ourselves "Never again!" But over time, the guilt and shame we feel associated with our past failings in this area build up inside of us once again, creating more of the same negative feelings we were attempting to escape. So we act out again. Thus, the addictive cycle has gone full circle and starts to repeat itself.

> *"Thank you so much for coming. I could really feel for everything you said . . . being a porn addict of six years. I really appreciate all you've said and I'm sure you've changed my life for the better."*
>
> ~ COMMENT FROM A MALE COLLEGE STUDENT

Guilt and shame. They are what propel the addictive cycle. So naturally, the degree of their presence in a person's life is a significant risk factor for sexual compulsivity and addiction. For this reason, several questions in the SAST pertain to guilt- and shame-producing sexual behaviors, both in terms of how they affect us (self-image) and how they affect others who are in relationship with us.

RELATIONAL CONSEQUENCES OF SEXUAL BEHAVIOR

When asked about the relational consequences of their sexual behavior, only a small percentage of our survey respondents reported that it was becoming an issue in their relationships with family, friends, or significant others.

> *"I didn't see my porn use as causing any problems in relationships and now I am able to identify some potential issues."*
>
> ~ COMMENT FROM A MALE COLLEGE STUDENT

The first question was, "Does your spouse (or significant other(s)) ever worry or complain about your sexual behavior?" Only 10% of the men and 7% of the women said "yes."

Then we asked, "Has your sexual behavior ever created problems for you and your family or friends?" Only 18% of the males and 14% of the females thought so.

On the surface, it might seem like these percentages should be higher given the many stories we all hear about how unwanted sexual behaviors have caused major problems in relationships and among family members. But this fairly low percentage of positive responses isn't surprising to me, and not just because it's likely that a large percentage of the students aren't married or in a committed relationship with a significant other. Several factors may be at work here: 1) a lot of families and couples aren't comfortable talking with each other about sexually related issues and even go out of their way to avoid those discussions; 2) most men and women have become pretty adept at hiding their sexual behaviors from others by the time they reach college age; and finally, 3) Addicts in the making are notorious for minimizing the effects their choices and behaviors are having on others.

> *"I just found out recently that my boyfriend struggles with porn. I can't begin to tell you how hurt I was and still am. I feel like he's been cheating on me this whole time."*
>
> ~ COMMENT FROM A FEMALE COLLEGE STUDENT

That last point is especially relevant to that small percentage of students who are already addicted or are edging ever closer to it. But for many, maybe even the majority of those who responded "no" to these questions, it could just as well be that their spouses, significant others, family members, and/or friends have simply accepted their sexual behavior as being perfectly normal, whether that involves abstinence or high levels of sexual activity.

> *"You really spoke true to me too because I have struggled with objectifying women in my life recently and I truly believe that it is because of the imagery that I have been exposed to in my life."*
>
> ~ COMMENT FROM A MALE COLLEGE STUDENT

What's also interesting here is the response to this related question: "Has anyone been hurt emotionally because of your sexual behavior?"

Quite a large percentage of both men and women admitted that their sexual behavior had indeed hurt others: 45% of the men and 42% of the women. So while nearly half of the students admitted to having hurt others close to them due to their sexual indiscretions, most of those same respondents also seem to think that it's not becoming an issue in those relationships. In light of this, we might assume that the amount of guilt and shame they're feeling as a result of these sexual behaviors is fairly low; especially since they appear to be getting away with whatever it is they're doing that's hurting other people. But instead of dealing with the sexual and relational issues before us, many respond by simply hiding. We hide from the fact that we know we're hurting ourselves and maybe even others. We also hide what it is that we're doing to ourselves and others because even when it's deemed acceptable or allowable by many of our peers, we know on a gut level that it's just not right. We know it's time to hide the facts and obscure the truth about what we're doing behind closed doors.

EMOTIONAL CONSEQUENCES OF SEXUAL BEHAVIOR

So do today's college students have anything they're doing sexually that they feel they need to hide from others, including their peers? When asked, "Do you hide some of your sexual behavior from others?" a whopping 58% of the college men and 52% of the college women said "yes."

> *"Great job with the personal story. Unfortunately, it awoke the hurt inside me from my parents' divorce and their similar situation."*
> ~ COMMENT FROM A FEMALE COLLEGE STUDENT

We then asked a related question, "Have you ever worried about people finding out about your sexual activities?" Again, over half of the men, 53%, and exactly half of the women, 50%, said "yes." Hiding our sexual behaviors from others because we're either too self-conscious or embarrassed to admit to them—especially if we've hurt others in the process—might seem somewhat normal. But doing so creates ideal conditions for guilt, shame, and self-hatred to take root. Having nothing to hide always works better, all the way around.

When we asked the students, "Do you ever feel bad about your sexual behavior?" 44% of the men and 39% of the women said "yes." In our current culture of postmodern sociosexual values that seems to regard its "no limits" tolerance of all things sexual among its greatest virtues, these high percentages of students saying "yes" surprised me. I'm convinced that sex is an inherently good thing, and that it can be a joyous and fulfilling experience for any couple as long as it's done within the context of what our creator God originally intended. A narrow view for some, I'm sure, but that is what I believe. Unfortunately, in part as a result of living in a hypersexual, pornographic culture that has commoditized sex for the sake of profit, very few of us seem to have a clear picture of what healthy sexuality looks like. I'm not even sure we can look back on our *Ozzie and Harriet* past and say that we ever did. We've either feared it or flaunted it—but how many of us really understand it and see it as the beautiful and potent gift that it is? But still we realize something's not right, and this is the first step toward getting back on track.

In yet another question directed at measuring sexual shame, we asked the students, "Have you ever felt degraded by your sexual behavior?" Here, a somewhat larger percentage of women than men said "yes"—33% compared to 29%. Still, roughly a third of all college students have felt degraded by their own sexual actions. In fact, about 12% of all college students (12% of the women and 11% of the men) even reported that they typically feel depressed after having sex.

Depressed! That's not exactly the next word that comes to most people's minds when you mention the words "college students" and "sex" together. But if you feel bad about your sexual behavior, even degraded by what you've done, and you and half of your peers are trying to hide your sexual behaviors from others while the other half is openly flaunting them, then it should come as no surprise that some young adults get depressed, if not confused, after having sex. We've failed them as

> *"Regardless of how many women I had sex with, it was never enough. It always left me feeling depressed, even guilty for breaking my own promises to myself to stop. It makes me feel like because of what I've done I'll probably never find the right girl and get married."*
>
> ~ COMMENT FROM A MALE COLLEGE STUDENT

87

sex educators—parents, teachers, pastors, and counselors alike—and in the process we've confused an entire generation about what it means to be a healthy sexual being. We've failed to paint them a picture of healthy sexuality, and we've failed to counter the culture's systemic distortion of sex and its objectification of men and women with an inspired vision that cares deeply about individuals, respects their rights, and seeks their well-being.

Instead, many of us adults, entrusted with the care and emotional health of our future generations, have abdicated our responsibility for being our children's primary source of sex education. As we struggle with our own issues of lust and sexual irresponsibility, or muddle along with our own feelings of guilt and shame over our past sexual indiscretions, we've left the door to the henhouse wide-open and thus invited the wolves among us to come in and dine.

THE CONSEQUENCES OF PORN CONSUMPTION

I remember reading with a certain amount of hesitation one blogger's review of my first book. In it, she was complimentary but especially critical of my overall treatment of the subject of pornography, implying that I was acting like a fear peddler and leaving part of her wondering if she shouldn't be looking over her children's shoulders every moment they spend online. Her belief was that not everyone struggles with pornography the way I did—which is true. That left her concluding that my views were alarmist and inconsistent with the fact that most people can actually enjoy porn without experiencing the dangers and consequences that I did.

After reflecting a while on her criticism and giving serious consideration to the idea that I had somehow lost my perspective on this issue, those closing words of hers hit me again. And every cell in my body reacted to the very thought—the distorted, faulty belief that I had fallen for so many years ago—that pornography had some redeeming value worthy of someone's time and attention. The idea that pornography, "sexually explicit pictures, writing, or other material whose primary purpose is to cause sexual arousal,"[1] could possibly be without harm or even beneficial to our society at large is a dangerous thought indeed.

In our society, pornography is widely regarded as a cheap, harmless form of entertainment—much like tobacco and cigarettes once were. No one thought anything about smoking back then; it was not only socially acceptable, it was also chic. We felt that way for many decades, thanks in part to the billions of dollars spent by advertisers glamorizing it on behalf of their clients. Then everything changed when we started noticing that a lot of our friends were dying of lung cancer and being crippled by emphysema and other diseases now linked to cigarette smoking. No doubt many perceived that smoking and these diseases were connected long before big tobacco producers were forced to admit it in courts of law. They had been lying to us for years, covering up the truth about how addictive cigarettes really were, and for a long time they got away with murder. Finally, when we started learning about the health risks of second-hand smoke, a lot of people got tired of breathing in other people's bad habit and started removing many of the rights we gave tobacco producers and smokers decades earlier that allowed them to light up in public places. In the end, the situation got out of hand as more and more people became addicted to this "harmless" form of rest and relaxation and *everyone* started sharing in the cost burden and consequences associated with smoking. Today, smoking is about as cool as clubbing seals and clearing rain forests.

"I have an addiction to pornography and it's lasted for many years. Hopefully, I will be strong enough to overcome it before it destroys my relationship with my girlfriend of three years. Thank you for sharing your struggles."

~ COMMENT FROM A MALE COLLEGE STUDENT

The social situation today as it relates to pornography reminds me a lot of the decline of smoking's popularity—from being an accepted form of personal relaxation, to one that was tolerated, to its present state as a socially unacceptable habit that's looked down upon and even legally discriminated against. Though porn has become the norm, I believe it too is on the verge of experiencing a societal backlash of sorts as millions find their lives negatively impacted by a close friend or family member who heavily consumes pornography. Whenever someone finds out what I do for a living (speaking out on the subject), it almost never fails that the next thing out of their mouth is a story about a spouse or child or friend who's losing their marriage or alienating friends because of their affinity for porn. Eventually, legal or not, people get fed up and start to demand change.

For those closer to my age, in their forties and fifties, the stories almost always involve a long, slow decline in marital or relational intimacy capped off by the sudden discovery of an Internet porn habit or other sexual acting out behavior long hidden from others until that individual could conceal it no longer. Somewhere along the line, their lives became unmanageable and they lost control of their hidden, unwanted sexual behaviors. Their private lives became public through a climactic event—an affair, arrest, job loss, or some other form of public disclosure and embarrassment that they couldn't keep hidden. Most by then had become addicts, unable to stop even in the face of severe consequences. And many, like myself, lost everything in the process—marriages, families, friends, careers, finances, reputations, and self-respect to name a few. Their addictive habit cost them everything, and almost all of them trace it back to the early development of that faulty belief system that pornography and all things pornographic embraces and exploits.

"Thank you. I'm forty-one, married fifteen years. I fight this addiction. I have two kids. I finally understand how porn works. God bless you!"

~ COMMENT FROM AN
    OLDER ADULT MALE

For those I meet in their twenties and thirties, their downfall has either come crashing down on them with alarming suddenness or it hasn't come at all—yet. But nearly all who have made porn consumption a regular part of their lives confess struggling in relationships. They talk about the guilt and shame they feel regarding sex and the difficulty they have experiencing genuine intimacy with others, sexual and nonsexual. Most of these people are living in the midst of what I call "sex syndrome," a preaddictive state where sex isn't satisfying because we've overstimulated ourselves to the point where we've become sexually desensitized. Don't believe it? Just talk with any advertising or marketing executive or creative director. They'll be the first to tell you of the difficulty they're having using sex to grab and hold the attention of today's consumer. Now that graphic sexuality is common in mainstream media and advertising, it takes more arousing pornographic images and edgier sexual messages than ever before to get your products noticed. This overdose of pop porn and exposure to ever more sexual images, especially those where sex and violence are combined, has affected the neurochemical tolerance levels of every consumer's brain to some degree (we'll see why in chapter 9).

In the scenarios I see that are so commonplace for those in their twenties and thirties, the quality of their relationships suffer from the very beginning. Those in their late teens and early twenties who enter committed relationships for the first time are often unprepared to handle true intimacy and fall hard. But they are also the easiest to help and usually have the best odds of fully recovering and even strengthening their marriages and relationships.

> *"I just wish my fiancé would've come. He needs to hear about this subject from someone other than me. I would like to know what you can do before your relationship hits rock bottom."*
>
> ~ COMMENT FROM A FEMALE
> COLLEGE STUDENT

Their fall is usually not precipitated by an addiction or hitting bottom as much as it is facing the reality of two conflicting belief systems for the first time. The faulty beliefs they've absorbed from porn don't match up to the needs of two people trying to establish and maintain a healthy, trusting, authentic relationship. So they frequently see the need to confess their past, confront their present inconsistencies, and choose to change their futures together with their partner. Their defining moment often comes early in the relationship and, as a result, the damage done tends to be minimal.

Most young couples I've met who had the courage to come clean and call a spade a spade (including sharing honestly their current sexual beliefs and behaviors and past sexual histories) have been able to move on and build stronger relationships. But those who don't, or feel like they can't, end up getting stuck in a cycle of repeating past relational failures, like so many older couples I've met who have justified similar decisions to hold onto their faulty beliefs at all costs. Call it stubbornness or blindness, their fate is sealed by their unwillingness to admit to past failures and right past wrongs. Whatever their motives and rationale, theirs is a guilt and shame-based existence. They're more established in their ways and have more at stake in changing their beliefs and thereby changing the direction of their lives. So much has been invested in this current path they're on that the thought of losing face before family and friends, of humiliating themselves before coworkers, and of possibly even having to start over is often too much for them to bear.

> *"I liked your willingness to be open about this struggle. This story has made me feel like I can love my girlfriend more so now."*
>
> ~ COMMENT FROM A MALE COLLEGE STUDENT

Instead of taking the hard way out by facing their demons, they consider the options, but are really only looking for ways to win without compromise. I sometimes find people like this in their late twenties, but it's commonplace for those in their thirties and early forties. They're still trying to have their cake and eat it too, convinced they can outsmart, outwit, and outplay the odds and the high probability that by continuing down the path they've chosen, they will certainly end up in a place they never really intended. They privately enjoy being players in this Porn Nation of ours, even though they continue to feel the need to hide their sexual beliefs and behaviors. Guilt and shame are factors they try to manage and control—and what better tool to do so with than their Great Escape? Yet the more time goes on, the more out of hand the scheme gets. They can't stop their declining capacity for sexual arousal. They can't reverse the damage done to their libido without turning up the volume on sexual stimuli to help compensate for the loss. These are addicts in the making, well on their way from sex syndrome to sexual addiction.

The longer we hang on to our faulty sexual belief system without challenging its precepts, the harder it is to recognize the truth about who and what we are as sexual beings. And the harder it is to forgive ourselves when we finally do see the truth from the lies. Nonetheless, it's a rite of passage that we all must face, regardless of our age. For to continue believing in the lies we tell ourselves means we're simply missing out on the very best that life and love has to offer us. We hold on tight to what we think is a life of sexual liberation and freedom, only to wake up one day realizing that we've lost control and have surrendered our freedom to others who don't care about our welfare and well-being. What a shock to think you're sexually liberated and free when you're really just a prisoner who's been locked up for years in a cage of your own making!

CHAPTER 9

WHO'S IN CONTROL HERE?

mericans have an interesting relationship with the word control. We seek to possess it, and fear losing it once we have it. Whether it's being "in control" of our lives (or the lives of others) or "taking control" of our own destinies, being in some state of control is something we all want. College students are no different. But when asked just how much control they feel they have over their sexual urges and desires, the picture they paint for us is truly alarming.

We asked college students several questions related to the matter of control, a key indicator of sexual compulsivity and addiction. Our first question read, "Do you have trouble stopping your sexual behavior when you know it is inappropriate?"

One in four college men (26%) said "yes" compared to nearly one in five women (18%). Both percentages seem high to me when you consider that these are students saying they're having a hard time stopping what they consider to be inappropriate sexual behavior. Their responses aren't just hypothetical. They're based on firsthand experience.

Sexual self-control is a problem for even more students who have said they actually tried to quit an unwanted sexual behavior and failed—38% of college men and 23% of college women. Many respond by trying to quit all forms of sex cold turkey after acting out. In fact, 29% of women and 27% of men we surveyed admitted they have times when they act out sexually followed by periods of celibacy (no sex at all). While we've already established that most of these respondents don't appear to be sex addicts, these are very common guilt- and shame-based practices among those who are. It's further evidence of a real battle being waged within one's own body, the flesh set against the mind and the spirit of an individual.

> *"Just like you, I've had no problem stopping masturbating to porn. I've done it a hundred times over."*
>
> ~ COMMENT FROM A MALE COLLEGE STUDENT

When the students we surveyed were asked who's in control of their sexual desires, the percentage of those admitting that they're losing this battle was also alarming, especially among college men. Nearly 1 in 5 men (19%) and 1 in 10 women (10%) acknowledged that they feel controlled by their sexual desire or fantasies of romance. One in four men (26%) and one in seven women (15%) have even thought that their sexual desires are stronger than they are.

> *"Thanks for speaking so openly about your struggle. I feel like I'm in a constant battle to control my thought life. Porn and sex is pretty wide open-on our campus, so it's like I face constant reminders everywhere I turn."*
>
> ~ COMMENT FROM A FEMALE COLLEGE STUDENT

Probably one of the most telling signs of the internal conflict raging within many students was their responses to the question, "Do you feel that your sexual behavior is not normal?" Again, a sizable percentage of college men (21%) and a slightly smaller percentage of college women (15%) said that they feel that their sexual behavior is not normal. What's really interesting about this question is we never attempt to define for the respondents what is normal or abnormal sexual behavior. They are answering this question based on what *they* consider to be normal sexual behavior, according to *their* own definition. Yet in spite of these many signs of problematic sexual behaviors and related issues with guilt, shame, and self-control, only 9% of the men and 4% of the women have ever sought help for sexual behavior they did not like. Overall, just 7% of the college students we surveyed are asking for help.

A big reason for this may be that only a small percentage of college students fit the clinical diagnosis of being sexually addicted. While indications of a struggle with unwanted sexual behaviors and self-control issues are definitely part of this disorder, only 1% of the 28,798 students we surveyed answered "yes" to 19 or more of the 25 core questions on the test. Those respondents are in the highest-risk group for their sexual behavior to interfere with and jeopardize important areas of their life (social, occupational, educational, etc.). In fact, many of them are probably already sexually addicted. But 1% is only a fraction of the overall national average of sexual addiction among adults, with best estimates said to be from 6% to 8% of the total population.[1]

Actually, the vast majority of college students we surveyed (77%) gave from 0 to 8 "yes" responses, putting them in the "low-risk" group, meaning that even though they may or may not have a problem with sexually compulsive behavior, the odds are in their favor that they don't and won't. The ones to really watch out for here, in addition to the high-risk students, are those who fall in the middle—the "at-risk" group. That group represents 22% of the students we surveyed, with 9 to 18 yes answers, putting them "at risk" for their sexual behavior to interfere with significant areas of their life. While it's likely that their sexual behaviors aren't yet jeopardizing important areas of their lives, there are definitely problem areas and enough signs that indicate they could easily be headed there.

When we combine the top half of those who are in the "at-risk" middle group with the "high-risk" group—that is, those respondents with 14 or more "yes" answers on the SAST—the result is that about 6% of all college students would probably be flagged by sexual addiction experts as problematic or potentially problematic and worthy of further testing and counseling. Since there have been no studies like this done in the past, it's hard to know for sure how many of those will struggle as sex addicts at some point in their lives. However, after students leave college and face a radically different environment as they enter the workplace, get into committed relationships, and start a family, it's reasonable to assume that many of those struggling with sexually related guilt and shame and self-control issues will experience an escalation of their unwanted sexual behaviors in the direction of sexual addiction. And most of those will be men.

> *"I grew up in a family where porn was always around. I just didn't think it was that big of a deal. But it's really hurt me in relationships. Now my fiancée isn't sure she wants to deal with all of this. But your story has given us hope."*
>
> ~ COMMENT FROM A MALE COLLEGE STUDENT

This becomes clear after further analyzing our respondents' total scores. While slightly more college men than college women (44% vs. 33%) made up the 77% of all students who fell into the low-risk group, men outnumbered women in both the at-risk and high-risk groups by a combined ratio of more than 2 to 1. Even when looking at those scoring above the median of 14 and above, men as a percentage made up over two-thirds of those who responded who are most likely to become sexually compulsive and addictive.

SAST RISK LEVELS	ALL	MEN	WOMEN
Low Risk (0-8)	77%	44%	33%
At Risk (9-18)	22%	15%	7%
High Risk (19+)	1%	<1%	<1%
Top Half (14+)	6%	4%	2%

While the consumption of pornography continues to grow among both men and women, companies in and out of the porn industry who use sex to sell us their products still cater mainly to men as their targeted customers. I believe the increased availability of pornography and the continued effort to normalize and mainstream pornographic attitudes, beliefs, and behaviors throughout our society has also prompted the onset of a new preaddictive state I call sexual compulsivity syndrome, or "sex syndrome" for short. And it's where many of today's college students are living.

SEX SYNDROME

By definition, sex syndrome is a pathological state we enter when our capacity for sexual pleasure and intimacy decreases as our exposure to intense sexual stimuli like cyberporn increases. It's a biological fact of life for both men and women, and taken to the extreme, it can result in sexual addiction.

To understand sex syndrome, you first need to have a basic understanding of how the brain, the most powerful sex organ in our body, processes sexual stimuli. We now know that there's a cocktail of chemicals in

> *"I don't think I'm addicted to porn, but I do have a real problem with it. Please help me."*
> ~ COMMENT FROM A MALE COLLEGE STUDENT

the brain that lights up lust and sparks romance.[2] In fact, those chemicals are totally different from the blend that fosters deep love and long-term attachment. One of the erotic chemicals is dopamine, a neurotransmitter that creates intense energy, exhilaration, focused attention, and motivation to win rewards. It's triggered by, among other things, novelty, pornography, and sexual arousal. Oxytocin is another chemical, actually a hormone, that promotes a feeling of connection, bonding, and attachment. It's produced and released by the brain when we hug our spouses or children, and when a mother nurses her infant. And there are others like serotonin and adrenaline that play more of a supporting role. But it's in this sandbox of love potions that pornography and its most toxic cousin, cyberporn, come to play.

Physiologically, in normal "love" relationships with real people, we typically move from the dopamine-drenched state of romantic love through various stages of increased intimacy to (if we're lucky) the relative calm and quiet of an oxytocin-rich attachment. But if we or our partners have formed a relationship with pornography (especially its more graphic forms) and use the material on a regular basis to induce fantasy-driven orgasms, our "relationship" with porn never leaves the attraction stage. It's always about a quick sexual high. So while porn repeatedly triggers intense sexual arousal, our brain keeps producing dopamine and stays stuck in an intense loop or cycle that mimics the early stages of infatuation, romance, and lovesickness. Overstimulate the brain with dopamine long enough, and the brain will adapt by adjusting and increasing its tolerance levels. But the result of increased tolerance is desensitization, similar to what an alcoholic or drug addict experiences after repeated use and abuse of his drug of choice.

> *"I've dealt with alcohol and drug addiction before I came to school here. But overcoming those addictions was a lot easier than dealing with my sex addiction."*
>
> ~ COMMENT FROM AN OLDER MALE COLLEGE STUDENT

Over time, as a user begins to require more sexual stimulation to get the same "high," they seek out new and different ways to increase the brain's production levels of dopamine. For the budding alcoholic or drug abuser, that may mean using greater quantities of the same drug or switching over to more potent drugs—beer to wine, wine to hard liquor, weed to cocaine—to get the same high as before. It works the same way for a sex addict in the making—magazines to videos, couple to group sex, from watching to becoming an active participant. In the meantime, the user sets, then crosses, boundaries; starts and promises to stop; then starts all over again. Sex syndrome is a scary place to be because you really don't think of yourself as being unhealthy or getting sick. You tell yourself and convince others that you're normal, that there's nothing wrong with it, that everyone's doing it. "It's harmless fun," you tell yourself, "nobody's getting hurt." But you can't see the long, slow slide. You're losing control but don't see what's really happening to you because you've developed blind spots in your behavioral awareness.

As you continue to feed the brain ever increasing amounts and varieties of intense sexual stimulation, the craving for a dopamine-drenched high grows. But the brain's ability to increase tolerance levels along the way to prevent overstimulation creates a quandary for the typical user. As he or she is surrounded with milder yet unsatisfying forms of sexual stimuli in our pornographic culture, they are constantly reminded of the need to quench their growing sexual appetite. The result is an ongoing sense of sexual dissatisfaction that can only be remedied by either a) suppressing or replacing a growing desire for sex, or b) seeking out new ways and methods of satisfying the sexual desire. As long as the relationship between experiencing sexual stimulation and achieving sexual satisfaction remains out of balance, the continued use of artificial sexual stimulants like pornography and out-of-bounds sexual behaviors (e.g., prostitutes, strip clubs, massage parlors, etc.) will only serve to increase sexual compulsivity.

The desensitization one experiences as tolerance levels increase comes as a result of overfeeding one's dopamine intake receptors. During this process the person is starving his capacity to experience healthy intimacy with someone in the context of a healthy relationship. Instead, his primary sexual relationship is either with an inanimate object like a picture or a video or a disengaged sex worker. Intimacy is what it's all about and for those struggling with sex syndrome, sexual intimacy has become all about taking without giving, which really isn't intimacy at all.

> *"Thanks for coming to speak at our campus. I've been struggling with porn ever since I was in high school, and your story has given me hope. I've tried to kick the habit, but it just never seems to go away."*
>
> ~ COMMENT FROM A MALE COLLEGE STUDENT

For many years now, psychologists and other medical experts in the field of sexual addiction and recovery have widely referred to sex addiction as an intimacy disorder. As a person becomes increasingly invested in a relationship with pornography, they are usually becoming more disconnected and isolated from others. It's a by-product of hiding their intentional and unwanted sexual behaviors from others. The messiness and "give-and-take" of real relationships has a hard time competing with the "all take-no give" false intimacy found in porn and casual sex. But the sense of satisfaction in false intimacy is short-lived.

As a person's sense of being fully known and accepted by others is being starved, their sense of self-esteem and significance decreases. In turn, the individual experiences even more isolation from real relationships. As sex syndrome gives way to sexual addiction and compulsivity, the unmanageability of it all starts to sink in and the shame and guilt that fuels the addictive cycle becomes well entrenched. Unhealthy sexual attitudes and behaviors not only skew the individual's moral and relational compass, but also become evidence of the need for self-condemnation based on the precepts of a faulty belief system.

"There's nothing wrong with porn. You were just a weak individual with poor self-control, so now you're blaming your addiction on porn. I use it all of the time and I'm not an addict."

~ COMMENT FROM A MALE COLLEGE STUDENT

While it's doubtful that sex syndrome will ever be recognized by the American Psychiatric Association as a mental disorder any more than they've been willing to acknowledge that sexual addiction exists, both are very tangible and real conditions for millions of people and their loved ones living in our Porn Nation. Most people who are experiencing the early and middle stages of sex syndrome see themselves as still in control of their lives and relationships. But if the latter stages of sex syndrome resemble a place where the fog is just starting to roll in and cloud their judgment and reasoning abilities, then sexual addiction is truly the place where they've lost all visibility.

For most college students, the idea of being addicted to anything is foreign and remote at their age. Deceived by their youthful sense of immortality into believing that they're immune to such dire consequences, many keep on marching toward danger, sure that they'll recognize the warning signs long before they're ever at risk. But sex syndrome isn't a destination, it's a pathway that all too often leads to a much darker place—sexual addiction. And in the chaotic world of sex addicts, the last thing they are is "in control."

CHAPTER 10

FROM SEX SYNDROME TO
SEX ADDICTION

On more than one occasion, a college student, after hearing my story, has come up and said something like, "Yeah, I was addicted to porn once for a while. But I got tired of it, so one day I stopped using it and it hasn't been a problem since."

My response: "If you could stop on your own, then you probably weren't addicted."

They always look surprised, even disappointed, when I say that. As if being a sex addict is the next cool thing and I've just cheated them out of all the fun and notoriety! With so many Hollywood stars and pop icons confessing addictions to one thing or another, and cycling in and out of cushy celebrity rehab-type recovery programs only to pronounce themselves completely cured after two weeks, who can blame them for being disappointed? I'm not sure how we got here, but somehow addiction and recovery got watered down and became chic at the same time. As Hollywood's elites and their publicists look to put the spin on one redemptive cover story after another, I'm convinced that most of these stories we hear or read about hardly resemble true recovery at all. Instead, they cheapen the severity of real addiction and leave those who truly struggle with unrealistic expectations about just how long and hard the path to recovery really is.

Also, while some high-profile social commentators like Oprah Winfrey repeatedly declare that sex addiction is America's number one addiction (and I happen to agree with her), some medical professionals and other people of influence still question whether sexual addiction even exists. In fact, the American Psychiatric Association, the organization that publishes the *Diagnostic and Statistical Manual of Mental Disorders* (or DSM), has yet to officially recognize sexual addiction as a mental disorder. That hurts the estimated sixteen to twenty-two million people in the U.S. who are sexually addicted[1] and their families, mainly because this guide is used by clinicians and researchers as well as insurance companies, pharmaceutical firms, and policy makers to help determine what mental disorders will be covered by medical insurance plans.

So while those affected by sexual addiction continue to battle the stigma attached to them by family and friends, those in the medical circles with the power to do something about it simply ignore it, much like they did sixty years ago with a little-known malady called alcoholism. Without its inclusion in the DSM, insurance companies who use this manual as a guide have been reluctant to provide insurance coverage to companies and their employees for a disorder they can claim doesn't officially exist.

WHAT IS SEXUAL ADDICTION?

So what is sexual addiction? Experts in the medical field who support its diagnosis describe it as being in many ways similar to other addictions, where the behavior or activity comes to be used as a way to manage mood or stress and may become more severe with time. Those like me and the sixteen to twenty-two million others (and our families and friends) who have lived through the nightmare and continue to live with the consequences have little doubt that sexual addiction is real and can be incredibly destructive.

Sexual addiction is among the least talked about and least understood of all addictions. Dr. Patrick Carnes, the world's foremost expert in the area of sexual addiction and recovery, defines sexual addiction as "any sexually related, compulsive behavior which interferes with normal living and causes severe stress on family, friends, loved ones and one's work environment."[2] It's also described as "a progressive intimacy disorder characterized by compulsive sexual thoughts and acts."[3]

> *"I have been exactly where your ex-wife has. Right down to considering driving my car into the tree. I am still married, but forever changed. Thank you for giving the greatest epidemic of our time a voice."*
> ~ COMMENT FROM AN OLDER ADULT FEMALE

Others talk about sexual addiction more in terms of having an unhealthy sexual dependency. The Mayo Clinic uses the phrase "compulsive sexual behavior" and defines it as having "an overwhelming need for sex." They describe someone with this behavior as "so intensely preoccupied with this need that it interferes with your job and your relationships. . . . You may spend inordinate amounts of time in sexually related activities and neglect important aspects of your day-to-day life in social, occupational and recreational areas. You may find yourself failing repeatedly at attempts to reduce or control your sexual activities or desires."[4] However you choose to define it, sexual addiction is seen universally as an unhealthy or pathological relationship between an individual and his sexual beliefs and behaviors.

> *"His road sounds somewhat familiar to where I'm headed. He helped me, thank you."*
> ~ COMMENT FROM A MALE COLLEGE STUDENT

The latest research in this field gives us a clearer picture of who sex addicts are. As mentioned, it's estimated that 3 to 6% of the U.S. population are sexually addicted. That adds up to about fifteen million people who suffer from this condition.[5] Other estimates put the number slightly higher at 6 to 8% of the U.S. population, or sixteen to twenty-two million people.[6] Either way, that's a lot of people—about the same number who struggle with alcoholism. They (we) come from every ethnic, religious, and socioeconomic background imaginable. Most sexual addicts also come from severely dysfunctional families. Dr. Carnes states that 87% come from a family where at least one other member has some kind of addiction. In addition, "Research has also shown that a very high correlation exists between childhood abuse and sexual addiction in adulthood." He notes that 97% of sexual addicts reported experiencing emotional abuse, 83% sexual abuse, and 71% physical abuse.[7]

While sexual addiction is generally assumed to be a condition primarily affecting men, research by Dr. Carnes shows that approximately 20–25% of all patients seeking help for sexual dependency are women. (This same male-female ratio is found among those recovering from alcohol addiction, drug addiction, and pathological gambling.) As once was the case with alcohol addiction, many people cannot accept the reality that women can become sexual addicts. One of the greatest problems facing female sexual addicts is convincing others that they have a legitimate problem.[8]

So how do you know if you or someone you love suffers from sexual addiction? While an actual diagnosis of sexual addiction should be made by a mental health professional, the following list of behavior patterns, composed by Dr. Patrick Carnes, are good indicators of sexual addiction. You can find this list and other helpful information on his Web site at www.sexhelp.com. You can also do what over twenty-six thousand college students have done and go to www.pornuniversitythebook.com to take the SAST.

Here are nine of the more common symptomatic behaviors associated with sexual addiction and compulsivity (for a more detailed explanation of sexual addiction, I recommend my first book on the subject, *Porn Nation: Conquering America's #1 Addiction*).

1. Acting out a pattern of out-of-control sexual behavior.
2. Experiencing severe consequences due to sexual behavior, and an inability to stop despite these adverse consequences.
3. Persistent pursuit of self-destructive behavior.
4. Ongoing desire or effort to limit sexual behavior.
5. Sexual obsession and fantasy as a primary coping strategy.
6. Regularly increasing the amount of sexual experience because the current level of activity is no longer sufficiently satisfying.
7. Severe mood changes related to sexual activity.
8. Inordinate amounts of time spent obtaining sex, being sexual, and recovering from sexual experiences.
9. Neglect of important social, occupational, or recreational activities because of sexual behavior.

As more and more of addicts' energy becomes focused on relationships that have sexual potential, other relationships and activities—family, friends, work, talents, and values—suffer and atrophy from neglect. Long-term relationships are stormy and often unsuccessful. Because of sexual overextension and intimacy avoidance, short-term relationships become the norm. Sometimes, however, the desire to preserve an important long-term relationship with spouse or children, for instance, can act as the catalyst for addicts to admit their problem and seek help.[9]

In my own life, I experienced every one of these behavior patterns at one time or another, and all of them simultaneously while I was addicted. Of course, at the time, I was in denial that they applied to me or were serious problems. But as the disorder progressively got worse, these behaviors became more pronounced to my family, friends, and loved ones, as did the related consequences. The existence of one or even a few of these behavior patterns could point toward any of a wide variety of causes or mental disorders. However, taken together as symptomatic behaviors in one individual, the probability that a sexual addiction exists is highly likely.

PATTERNS OF SEXUAL ADDICTION

Before getting help, most addicts have tried often to stop on their own and have failed. Their behavior generally conforms to a repetitive pattern or cycle that most find themselves unable to break out of.[10]

PREOCCUPATION — The addict becomes completely engrossed with sexual thoughts or fantasies. When asked the question, "Do you often find yourself preoccupied with sexual thoughts or romantic daydreams?" about two-thirds of all college students responding to our survey said that they did. The percentage of college women who often find themselves preoccupied with such thoughts wasn't that much different from the percentage of college men. Some of this overwhelming response is predictable as college-aged students have always been known for their raging hormones. But never before has it been so easy to feed those sexual urges in extreme ways and remain anonymous and totally hidden from others.

> "I was a crystal meth addict and I spent days and days obsessing over porn. I would look at it for eight, nine hours a day. I can relate to everything you talk about."
>
> ~ COMMENT FROM A MALE COLLEGE STUDENT

RITUALIZATION — The addict follows special routines in a search for sexual stimulation that intensifies the experience and may be more important than reaching orgasm. Many rituals are commonplace in the life of a college student. Classes and social events appear on their schedules like clockwork. But perhaps their most ritualistic behaviors have to do with their interactions with technology. Just walk around Porn University and you'll see the mass of heads-down texting going on or cell phones pressed against students' ears, creating a chorus of partial dialogues. Others walk around attached to their earphones and iPods, immersed in their music. Every once in a while, you actually notice students walking together and talking to each other. Now I don't mean to be critical here, but I'm amazed at how it's become totally acceptable behavior to be publicly zoned out and tuned in to whatever tech-driven device is holding one's attention at the moment. And with wireless porn getting amped up and ready for prime time on the latest 3G network devices, the presence of hi-res, streaming-video "porn in your pocket" will soon be commonplace. A new application has entered a world where well-established rituals already exist.

COMPULSIVE SEXUAL BEHAVIORS — This is the addict's specific sexual acting out behaviors. Examples include compulsive masturbation, indulging in pornography, having chronic affairs, exhibitionism, dangerous sexual practices, prostitution, anonymous sex, compulsive sexual episodes, and voyeurism. By the time they reach college, most students today have already demonstrated a high capacity for, if not a history of, compulsivity. Just watch your average gamer or avid fan of text messaging, or just about any student glued to the latest episode of their favorite TV program or Web-based application (Facebook, YouTube, etc.).

Technology providers and application developers have been striving for years to increase the "stickiness" of their infotainment offerings. They're trying to get us glued to whatever it is they're offering, especially if it's on the Web. By its very nature, Internet porn accomplishes this better than most online applications. With banner ad come-ons

> *"You see porn on just about every computer screen in nearly every male dorm room on campus. I just graduated a few years ago, but I think I'd have a hard time being a student today in that kind of environment. It's just everywhere and totally accepted as a normal part of campus life."*
>
> ~ COMMENT FROM AN ADULT MALE COLLEGE ADMINISTRATOR

and click-thru's generating more and more revenue for all involved, commercial Web site pornographers have perfected the art of enhancing their compulsivity factor to the degree that Internet porn now ranks as one of the most addictive forms of sexual addiction. They have also found ways

> *"Yeah, sure, everyone looks at porn. In fact, my boyfriend and I use it all the time."*
>
> ~ COMMENT FROM A FEMALE COLLEGE STUDENT

to replicate nearly every form of sexual acting out behavior mentioned above. Thus to wander into the world of cybersex is to flirt with what experts in the field refer to as the "crack cocaine" of sexual addiction. And for that large percentage of college students with a sexual history that puts them at risk of developing problematic sexual beliefs and behaviors, they're playing a game of Russian roulette with their future hopes and dreams that many of them will eventually lose.

DESPAIR — The acting out does not lead to normal sexual satisfaction, but to feelings of hopelessness, powerlessness, and depression. Risk factors for the addict include unstructured time, the need for self-direction, and demands for excellence, because they all push the addict toward restarting the addictive cycle. The feelings of guilt, shame, and despair that many college students admittedly struggle with will be the very things that keep them trapped in the addictive cycle. Immediately after acting out, these students will despise themselves for what they have done and promise themselves to never do it again. But in order to evade those intense negative feelings of self-hatred and disgust, they will seek to escape by becoming preoccupied with a whole new series of sexual thoughts and fantasies. There is always a trigger or false hope that will con them into thinking that this time their Great Escape will do the trick and finally take away their pain or boredom for good.

This is the sorry existence of the sex addict. Over time, their despair can easily turn to hopelessness as their continued efforts to stop the addictive cycle fail them. For some, these feelings of powerlessness bring them back to childhood experiences of sexual, physical, or emotional abuse. For others, this is a new feeling that many will fight to the end in a battle of willpower. But for those caught up in the addictive cycle and unable to break out on their own, reaching out and asking for help from others is the only way most will survive. For all but a very small percentage of college students, asking someone for help with their unwanted compulsive, addictive sexual behaviors will be a totally new and humbling experience.

> *"I've been beating myself up over this problem for years now. Tried recovery groups, counseling, prayer, medications. Nothing seems to work. Help! What do I do next?"*
>
> ~ COMMENT FROM A MALE COLLEGE STUDENT

Sure, sexual addiction is controversial, and it is important to realize that some people grab onto this label as an excuse or a crutch instead of accepting personal responsibility for the choices they've made in life, choices that may have hurt themselves and others. Many college students feel that older adults use labels like "sex addict" as a crutch or a scapegoat, and for that reason many of them still remain skeptical that such a thing really exists. But the truth is sexual addiction or sexual compulsivity or whatever you want to call it is a very stark reality for millions of men and women. For some, it's a living hell that instills intense feelings of hopelessness and helplessness in the face of an onslaught of pornographic images and messages fed to us in our media-driven culture. For those of us on the other side of recovery, it's a very real mountain that we had to climb that has left us with unforgettable scars and bruises.

> *"I was a girl searching for love in all the wrong places, dressing to get attention. Even if it was negative, it was better than nothing. I had always felt empty and alone."*
>
> ~ COMMENT FROM A FEMALE COLLEGE STUDENT

Few college students have lived long enough and experienced enough of life itself to truly appreciate that they could fall victim to their own reckless disregard for the power of sexuality. They don't yet fully understand or appreciate that sexuality is more than just skin deep. For those among us who are older and wiser, it's understood to be a very fragile, very human form of intimacy with others. But for many students I meet (and older adults who refuse to grow up), the goal for them isn't intimacy with others. They just want to feel good. They just want to have sex.

So what is it that they really want? Is it sex, or is it intimacy? To be noticed, or to be more fully known?

XXX

GRADUATE STUDIES

CHAPTER 11

BEING KNOWN OR
BEING NOTICED?

All too often we discover our weaknesses and become self-aware much too late in the game. By then we've damaged ourselves and inflicted pain on others. As this reality sets in, so does the guilt and shame, and suddenly we find there's no one left to blame but ourselves.

One night after I gave my Porn Nation talk at a university, a rather brazen student came up to me and said matter-of-factly, "Mr. Leahy, you talked about how we're all seeking intimacy." I wasn't really sure where he was going with this until he startled me with his next statement. "Well, I don't really care about intimacy. I just want to have sex!" While I appreciated his boldness and honesty, I was saddened by his naiveté. But it got me thinking—do today's college students really know how deeply interwoven sex and intimacy are, or at least are supposed to be? And can they see how they're being sold on the "importance" of being noticed versus the *significance* of being known?

Thinking back on it, I'm sure when I was his age I'd have responded much the same way—and I would have been absolutely, positively honest in my response. In college, it was all about feeling good, even if it made me look bad to some. But while I was in hot pursuit of my hedonistic pleasures, I actually preferred just being noticed over being known because there were things about myself I needed to hide from others. In fact, the last thing I really wanted was for someone to really "know" me since I was convinced that if anyone did, they wouldn't love me or want to have anything to do with me. I was terrified of being known, and I suspect a lot of college students today still feel that way as evidenced by their responses on our sex survey. Based on these students' responses, the consumption of pornography and the sexual attitudes and actions it inspires sound anything but "harmless" to me.

So is it really possible that today's students don't really know what they want when it comes to sex, love, and relationships? That's possible. But I think the survey results have shown us that the more likely scenario is that they *do* know what they want (and it is intimacy), but the problem is they're simply going about the wrong way to get it. Today, most college students seem very much like many of their counterparts across the wide spectrum of our society—they want to have it all. In the area of relationships, there's a battle that's raging and it's pushing the possibility of true intimacy right off the table for many students. In today's digital world of social networking on a global scale and what I'll call "assumed anonymity" (assuming that one's online behaviors are untrackable and anonymous, when they really aren't), the battle is between seeking to *be known* (relational intimacy) and trying to *be noticed* (popularity and celebrity). Unfortunately, the latter usually trumps the former.

For one, intimacy for many college students is synonymous with the physical act of sexual intercourse. At a deeper level, however, intimacy refers to a closeness and familiar understanding and knowledge of someone. A simple way I like to think of it and explain it to students is like this: break it down, and intimacy is like IN-TO-ME-SEE. In other words, true intimacy in a relationship is all about being fully known and knowing another more fully, and not necessarily in a sexual or physical sense. That person sees and knows all of you from the inside out. He or she sees into you, and vice versa. This is much more than skin deep or surface-level knowledge about a person. If relationships define the essence of humanity, then intimacy in relationships, especially nonsexual intimacy, is at the core of our well-being. Nothing can make us feel more connected than being fully known and appreciated by another, and knowing that person fully as well.

But what happens when we're burdened with guilt or shame or when we have something to hide? Such burdens erode our capacity to experience true intimacy with others. We can't be fully known because there's always a secret to keep, some part of ourselves that we feel we must hide from others. That was a recurring theme we noticed throughout the responses to our survey questions for a significant number of students. And it's a strong indicator that when it comes to this beautiful thing we know as our God-given sexuality, many of us are still walking around with a tarnished and distorted picture of what it really means to be a healthy and flourishing human being, made in the image of God.

Throughout college and for the next twenty years, I hid my true self from others, even those closest to me like my wife, my family, and my best friends. Regardless of their best efforts to get to know me, I could never be transparent and allow myself to be fully known because I was too worried about what would happen if anybody really knew everything about me. The idea of having those sexual thoughts and attitudes that I entertained behind closed doors later discovered by others left me fearful of being rejected, abandoned, or considered unlovable. So I kept that part of me locked away in a secret world to which I alone held the key. Such an existence is the antithesis of true intimacy or being fully known. In order to keep things hidden from others, I learned to create a "false intimacy" with those closest to me—my wife, my kids, my family—by posing and lying. I fed them an image of what I thought they were looking for while simultaneously holding back the most intimate parts of who I really was, including my fears and emotions that I was constantly trying to escape from. So I used porn, my drug of choice, to numb the pain. Of course, that only led to a further disintegration of who I really was until I could no longer keep the two worlds apart. The result was a stunned circle of family and friends discovering my sexual addiction as a result of learning about my affair with another woman. They just couldn't believe that there was a Mr. Hyde lurking beneath my Dr. Jekyll public persona all this time.

> *"My dad had a problem with pornographic material! That almost cost his family, but I hope he's over it. I pray that he is."*
> ~ COMMENT FROM A FEMALE COLLEGE STUDENT

While it might be true that a relatively small percentage of the college students we surveyed struggles with the day-to-day turmoil of sexual addiction, a considerably larger percentage admitted to hiding their sexual behaviors from others, worrying about being found out by others, feeling degraded and abnormal, and even being unable to control their sexual desires. Sexual shame and guilt was a recurring theme throughout our results, as was the fear of being discovered. Yet many of today's students continue to publicly display what a lot of people consider to be outlandish and pornographic sexual attitudes, beliefs, and behaviors. Does this contradiction mean our numbers are off, or is there something else going on here that we're missing?

THE NEW PORNOGRAPHERS

Real intimacy in relationships, being fully known and knowing others, is hard work. It's also risky. There's the possibility of being misunderstood, mistrusted, suffering hurt feelings, or being flat out rejected by others. If being loved and accepted *by others* is your main goal, then being transparent and vulnerable to them may seem like a risky proposition indeed. However, if your primary goal is the selfless love and acceptance *of others*, seeking first to understand *them* rather than to be understood, you have a much better chance of experiencing a deep and abiding level of intimacy in relationships with others. The problem for many of today's college students is they are so caught up in the societal hype and constant pressure of being noticed that there's much less interest in being known.

There are a lot of reasons for this, I'm sure. Some of it is certainly rooted in their baby boomer parents' (that's me and my peers) penchant for acquiring the stuff of status and celebrity. We collectively sought out recognition and material wealth at the expense of relational riches and closer family ties. The gadgets and time-savers of life like cell phones, PDAs, cable TV, DVDs, and wireless Internet all fed our insatiable craving for instant gratification, whether that meant tracking stock prices or indulging in theater-quality home entertainment. Then our equally insatiable appetite for all things celebrity gave rise to the reality show and the idea that you no longer had to be a real celebrity to be a celebrity. Everyday people could now script their fifteen minutes of fame with greatly increased odds of seeing it actually happen. Whether you appear on network TV, a cable news program, YouTube, Facebook, MySpace, or on your own podcast or blog, being noticed has become the name of the game. In the social networking world, how many "friends" you have linked to your site still carries more weight for some people than what a person actually has to say or who they really are. These large numbers of strangers and acquaintances mislabeled as "friends" gives the illusion of acceptance and popularity, even celebrity, among those living in the upper echelons of connectedness.

So how does one stand out and get noticed in the midst of a crowded field, say eighty million Facebook users? One way is to do what commercial advertisers and marketers learned long ago—you go pornographic. By exposing everything but sharing nothing, you transcend notoriety and become a novelty instead. That's because porn is no longer taboo in our anonymous digital world. Unless you're a known celebrity, your value in the buff is based solely on your body shape and size, and possibly your sexual acumen. In other words, the more you look and act and sound like a porn star, the higher your stock is likely to rise—for a while, that is, until the next pretty face shows up. And while you may not be able to strut your stuff in the buff on Facebook, there are many other ways to accomplish that on the digital frontier.

Today the message our students get is that it's all about the wrapping on the package. No one really cares about what's inside anymore. No one really wants to know you, and they certainly don't want to be known themselves. As our test results have shown, they're too busy hiding who they really are—including their penchant for pornography—from their girlfriends or boyfriends, spouses, parents, or employers. On the Internet, whether in pictures or prose, the nearly anonymous exchanges that take place always seem to devolve into a sexualized, objectified dialogue where you're never really sure who (if anyone) in the conversation is telling the truth. Yet millions do the dance every day, seeking out something they don't yet possess but offering little in return. These are the widely followed principles of consumption in our Porn Nation where taking is expected and giving is rare, and where anonymity creates the illusion of safety while acting more like a house of mirrors at the midway.

Some who are as adept at playing the game as I once was are now joining the ranks of what I refer to as the "new pornographers." Their motive isn't profit but rather celebrity, or at least recognition and acceptance from their peers. Instead of entertaining themselves by watching commercial pornographers use washed-up porn actresses donning pigtails and posing as "the girl next door," these new pornographers are actually shooting video of the girl who lives next door, with or without her permission. In other words, they're beating the industry giants at their own game by playing by a totally different set of rules. Those who are equally motivated, but are more "behind-the-scenes" kinds of guys, concentrate on managing the data repositories for their exhibitionist peers. And of course, in this new world of reality porn, the talent pool for both is vast.

My first experience in learning about this trend came several years ago while speaking at the University of California at Santa Barbara. After giving my talk, several students came up to me and asked me if I had met "the porn guy" yet. I assumed they were referring to one of their friends nearby. Instead they told me about a guy on campus whom they'd never met but was already legendary to the other students. His celebrity came as a result of operating the largest shared network porn server on campus. Back then he had over a terabyte of pornographic pictures and movies loaded on his computer, including, I'm sure, a lot of pirated content, much to the dismay of the commercial porn industry. Through the use of free and fairly common shared network services software, every student on campus who wanted it had 24/7 access to this massive porn server and all of its content. Thus, he was looked upon as a hero of sorts by his pro-pornography classmates.

I'm sure by now that every Porn University has at least a few "porn guys" and a whole host of porn-guy wannabes. Just as alarming though is the large number of college women and men who won't hesitate to expose themselves to millions of strangers online for decades to come by appearing in homemade porn videos or on sexually oriented Web sites, many of their own making. This blatant exhibitionism creates an appetite for voyeurism and the further sexual exploitation of women, men, and children. The damage this kind of self-abuse does to the individual(s) involved is both far-reaching and nearly impossible to quantify at this early stage of their lives. The bulk of the damage won't occur until several years down the road, much like it hit the hardest in later years for me. The erosion of self and objectification of others can be a long, slow process. But it will eventually come to those who are deeply involved and invested in the making and consumption of porn.

CHANGE CAN START LONG BEFORE COLLEGE

As the survey results have shown us, a foundation of sexual shame and guilt already exists among today's college students, as does a history of unwanted sexual behavior in the face of a growing inability to control their sexual urges and desires. For those of us who have traveled down this road before, it's frustrating to see others pass us by without heeding our warnings. But instead of trying to save the world, many of us would better serve our nation and our families and friends by focusing more on trying to reach our own children. We all have a vested interest in seeing our kids turn out well, so when it comes to sensitive personal subjects like sex, love, relationships, and pornography, most of us would prefer that our children learn about these things from us rather than from strangers. In fact, I would love for that to be the reason that I go out of business and am no longer needed to speak to college students about these subjects. However, after spending a lot of time talking with the parents of teens and college students, it's become apparent to me

> *"I was craving this—I have been grappling with sex and spirituality for a long time and you have helped illuminate some truths. Thank you."*
>
> ~ COMMENT FROM A MALE COLLEGE STUDENT

that most of us who are parents don't really know how to talk with our kids about these subjects. As a result, our silence is deafening to an entire generation of kids with a lot of questions on their minds about their sexuality.

After speaking to so many college students, you'd think it would be easy for me to sit down and talk with my two boys about these matters. But the truth is I still struggle in that role of sex educator just like most parents I've talked to. Even though I've educated myself on the hidden dangers and long-term consequences of porn consumption, which I also personally experienced, and even though I know all of the studies and statistics that go along with my thesis, I still find myself struggling to have those honest, healthy conversations with my boys. I'm discovering that my difficulties have more to do with my own shortcomings than they do with their unwillingness to discuss the subject matter. Sometimes, in order for others to trust us and believe in what we say and do, we first have to learn to trust ourselves. Likewise, while we may have even matured to the point where we can freely and easily forgive others, oftentimes we limit our ability to connect with others and experience true intimacy because we've never really forgiven ourselves. Until we're able to forgive ourselves of the mistakes of our past and trust that we'll say and do the right thing around our kids, they'll have a hard time believing us and trusting our conviction.

So how do we get there from here? And is there anything we can start doing today that will help better equip us for those teachable moments in the future? The answer is yes, we can turn the tide and break the chains of sin and silence that have shackled many of us when it comes to really understanding who we are as relational and sexual beings. First, however, we need to make sure we know what it is that our children, especially our older, college-aged kids, really want and need, even when they're not sure what it is.

CHAPTER 12

WHAT
EVERY STUDENT
REALLY WANTS—
AND NEEDS

The first time I shared my story with a trusted friend outside of my recovery group, I had been in recovery for several years and had developed a burning desire to help others who struggled. I thought that by sharing my story and the wisdom I had acquired along the way with others they might find the hope and help they needed to get well. This friend urged me to tell my story by writing a book. When I reminded him that I had never written a book before and wasn't really sure that I could, he gave me some advice to help me find my way: "Don't think about writing a book. Instead, just start writing as if you're writing a letter to your boys."

What a great idea, I thought. I need to use my writing ability and write down my honest thoughts and feelings in a letter to my boys anyway. That was six years and two books ago and I still haven't written that letter. My wife, Christine, reminds me often of the many promises I've made to myself to write it. But I've always found some sorry excuse to put it off. The truth is, sharing the deepest part of me with my boys has always loomed large, like some Herculean task. I think it's interesting that while I can pour my heart and soul out to total strangers, whether one-on-one or before millions of people on national TV, I still struggle with the idea of facing my own kids with the truth about who I really am. Oh, we've talked about stuff plenty of times before on a surface level. You know, what I did at work that day, what they did at school that day, wondering who's going to win the Super Bowl. I know they've read articles about me, seen and heard me telling my story—our story—on TV. We've even had our moments where the connection went deeper than that, talking about their relationships and stuff I already know about that's going on in their personal lives. But I never really ask them about what they're feeling, how their heart is, how sex and love and relationships and porn are affecting them. Odd, don't you think?

The difficulty of navigating these precious waters has changed much for me over the years. I've tried to stay involved in their lives since their mom and I were first separated in 1997. With eleven years of hard work at recovery under my belt, I've been able to enjoy a much healthier relationship with them even though we never seem to spend enough time together. (They moved away with their mother shortly after our divorce and her remarriage.) But even with the time we're afforded, I find myself all too often initiating conversations and responding to them more like my dad used to do with me, rather than how I've always wanted it to be with them and him. My dad was visibly uncomfortable about the subjects of love, sex, relationships, and especially porn. Who can blame him? I'm sure his parents weren't much better at it either. Yet I've learned to open up to strangers in a way that's honest and authentic and vulnerable. Why is this so hard for me now?

I got a clue as to why recently. I was listening to the pastor of my church, Andy Stanley, as he talked about the unique dangers and consequences that accompany sexual sin. Reflecting on his many years spent talking with students in student ministry and now counseling couples as a senior pastor, he remarked how people who had fallen into sexual sin all seemed to share one thing in common that was unlike everyone else's struggle with other types of sin—they had the hardest time forgiving themselves. Later he explained, "People who have cheated on their spouses and been unfaithful to their wives or husbands often have intimacy issues with their adult children. That wasn't their intention going in, but adult children develop trust issues with unfaithful parents every time. As a result, the unfaithful parent has given up much of their *moral authority* and influence in their children's lives."

Wow! That one hit me right between the eyes. It impacted me because I've started to see it in my own life. Many, many times I have looked into the eyes and hearts of my two boys over these past eleven years and noticed a sadness and a check in their spirit toward me. It's not that I believe they don't love me or haven't forgiven me. I know they do and have many years ago. However, I do believe that no matter how hard I try, and no matter how much I do to try to reverse the damage, that the consequence of mistrust is and always will be present to some degree. For that reason, along with many others, the greatest challenge I face every day is always to truly forgive myself for what I've done.

> *"My parents separated over my father's porn addiction; your story has helped me start to forgive and love my father."*
>
> ~ COMMENT FROM A FEMALE COLLEGE STUDENT

THE PATH TO FORGIVENESS

So what do you do about that as a parent? And what can you do as the child of an unfaithful parent? What if you're now the adult and your past struggles with trusting a parent have seeped into your current relationships? How do you learn to trust again? What will it take to free yourself from this guilt and shame heaped onto you by someone you once trusted? These are difficult questions, and depending on your past circumstances, they can actually become debilitating and hijack your life. They can lead you down a path of depression, anxiety attacks, and a deep sense of loss and unhappiness.

Which brings me to the big question posed by this chapter's title: Do you know what every student *really* wants and needs? I thought I did when raising my two boys, but it took losing everything—my marriage, family, friends, job, and reputation—and then sharing my story with college students for the past six years before I found out. It's all summed up in what I call "the two big questions" students ask *every time* in the Q&A portion of my Porn Nation presentation:

1) How's your relationship with your ex-wife?
2) How's your relationship with your boys?

Still not sure about the answer yet? Well, as I've fielded these two questions over and over again, and as I've closely observed both the student asking the question and the silence that takes over the room the moment these questions are asked, two words constantly come to mind: *reconciliation and restoration.* That's what every student at Porn University is really looking for—a reason to have *hope for reconciliation and restoration* in their own relationships, especially with their parents.

These students are hurting deep down inside. I'm convinced that many if not all of them to some degree are the products of broken or badly damaged relationships with their own parents. They've heard my story, and they've felt the pain from a different perspective—that of the affected child. While some can identify with my addiction story, *all* can identify to some degree with my boys and ex-wife. And many of them are still bearing the scars of the consequences of their father's or mother's failings or sin. Whether it led to divorce or separation or left a lingering sense of distance and abandonment in a family still barely intact, they *all* desire the same thing: healing, reconciliation, and restoration of the most important relationships in their lives—their relationships with their parents, and just as important, their parents' relationship with each other.

This is something I wrestled with in my own life after getting divorced.

My relationship with Patty was anything but civil for many years after our divorce. As a result, my relationship with my boys suffered and was often full of tension and conflict, mirroring my relationship with their mom. Yet I now understand that a lot of that anger and resentment that I used to feel toward her, both while we were married and after we were divorced, was deeply rooted in my own insecurities and inability to forgive myself for who I thought I was and what I was becoming.

One thing that I learned through recovery that has helped me the most in overcoming the sense of shame, guilt, and unforgiveness that I've felt for so long is to view myself and my life in the context of how the God of the Bible sees it, and in what He has to say about *our* relationship (God and me). In other words, if I'm feeling sad or stressed out about some aspect of my relationship with myself or another person, and especially with my wife or my boys, I try to turn to God first to see how things are between us (again, God and me). Nine times out of ten I find the problem is inside of me and has little to do with anyone else. But I've learned from past mistakes that it's sometimes hard to see around our blind spots in a way that we can really see the truth about ourselves. That's where Jesus comes in. Without knowing the fact that Jesus once lived and walked the face of this earth as fully man and fully God, it would be hard for me to trust God. I mean, how could He really know how I feel without having experienced life on earth in the person of Jesus Christ? But since Jesus has walked in my shoes and felt my pain, and understands what rejection and suffering is all about, I walk today with a renewed sense of confidence. I know that my sins have been forgiven, and my personal redemption story serves as evidence of that and the fact that God has a plan and purpose for my life—in spite of my shortcomings.

I didn't always feel that way about God. Before I started to trust God and relate to Him through a personal relationship with Jesus Christ, my concept of God was that He was more like a reflection of my earthly father, whom I loved but mostly feared. But Jesus Christ made it all personal. His presence in my life made God relatable to me for the first time ever. As I read His story in the Bible and started to really pay attention to what He said and what He did and who He claimed to be, it all started to make sense to me. Slowly but surely I started to recognize that Jesus Christ's presence on this earth was meant to direct all of mankind's attention to reconciliation with His and our heavenly Father. Jesus' character and compassion and healing power, and especially His capacity to forgive and restore broken relationships, was simply meant to serve as an illustration of who His Father is and what His Father is all about. I now realize that my perfect heavenly Father is completely different from my earthly father, who loved me but was flawed and fallible.

Several years ago, a dear friend and wise Christian counselor shared with me and the others in my sexual addiction recovery group a powerful illustration of the difference Christ makes in relationships. Our discussion that night centered on our frustration with how to navigate the choppy waters of forgiveness and trust after what we had done. Finally, after going back and forth for much of the night, a member of the group challenged him to respond to one of our greatest fears: "How can we ever trust ourselves again in relationships?" After hesitating for a moment, this man we all thought we knew so well began to share a painful part of his story most of us had never heard before. It turned out that early in his marriage he was a serial adulterer. His wife hadn't just endured his porn habit or an affair with another woman but years of multiple affairs with many women. As I listened to him tell the story, I started to wonder what was wrong with his wife. I mean, how could she stick it out so long with a guy like him? Regardless of the reasons for his wife's endurance, we were all dying to know how she did it. How did she learn to ever trust him again?

"It was quite simple, really," our mentor went on to explain. "When I asked her the same question many years later, she answered, 'I knew I could never trust you again. But I could trust Christ in you. So as long as I saw evidence of Him in you, I was okay.'"

A few years after our divorce, I heard a very similar response from my ex-wife, Patty. "The boys and I have noticed you've changed quite a bit," she once said. "You're a different man than you used to be—much kinder, much calmer." We both knew why since both of us were Christians and knew that I had chosen to return to my relationship with God after abandoning Him many years earlier.

Even though God has used my failings and this experience to change me from the inside out, there is still much more work to be done. But it was in the midst of that storm of brokenness and humility that I experienced God starting to do something I could never do for myself. He started to restore and reconcile my relationships, first with my ex-wife, Patty, then with my boys, and later with many other significant people in my life—her family, my own brothers and sisters, even Patty's husband, a man whom I unjustifiably hated and resented for many years.

The students I speak to had sensed this. Maybe it was seeing video clips of Patty and me sharing our story together on *20/20* or *The View* with national TV audiences. Or maybe it was seeing the tears flowing from my eyes whenever I spoke of the consequences of lost time and memories with my boys. Whatever the reason, they always ask those two big questions. Interestingly, now that I've remarried, the question "How's your relationship with your new wife?" has started to appear just as frequently.

It may have taken me a while to get here, but I've had plenty of life lessons by now that have taught me that even when I feel inadequate to speak the truth about love, sex, relationships, and porn to my kids, I can at least speak with confidence and assurance when I'm sharing with them what I've been learning about God's plan and design for my life and who He says we are as sexual beings. When I turn to God's Word for direction, I always discover a wealth of wisdom and sound advice that

> *"My father is on a similar path as you. He's had affairs . . . and has a porn/sex addiction. I wish you could speak to him before our family is broken."*
>
> ~ COMMENT FROM A FEMALE COLLEGE STUDENT

usually runs counter to what I grew up believing. This priceless knowledge helps me tremendously when I'm searching for the right words to say to my kids. But unlike the stoic apologist we've all met who goes around quoting Scripture verse after Scripture verse without truly risking himself or being vulnerable in the process, my approach has always been to make it more personal—thinking through some of the applications of God's truth in my own life that I learned from and could eventually share with others.

I wish I could say this thought process always resulted in having engaging, honest conversations about who I really am with my boys, but I can't. Why? Because I've been afraid—afraid of looking less than fatherly, of being considered weak, of appearing like a failure, or worse yet, believing myself to really be one. The poser and phony in me is always lurking just around the corner, waiting for me to invite him back onto the main stage of my life. But I've also learned my lessons the hard way, so that is an old acquaintance that will never be welcomed back into my life again.

As I've come to this place in my book, it's true that I've been saddened by this tendency in my life, and the resulting missed opportunities and teachable moments with my boys that I've let slip by. So today, I've decided to take a small step forward and write that letter to my boys. For writing is the one thing I know how to do. What I'm going to say exactly, I have no idea at this moment. But I'm convinced that waiting for just the right words and the right time is part of what's paralyzed me to this point. So perhaps it's just better to start writing. Something. Anything. As long as it is true and honest and from the heart. That I know I can do.

CHAPTER 13

A LETTER FROM DAD

Dear Chris and Andrew,

I realize this might seem kind of strange, reading a letter from your dad written in a published book for all to read. But there are some things I know I need to say to you both that I'm afraid many other fathers may not be able to say to their kids even though I'm pretty sure they want to deep down. I kind of know how they feel. After all, look at how long it's taken me to write this!

First of all, I want you both to know how sorry I am for cheating on you. I'm not sure I've ever quite put it that way before. But I realize now that I wasn't just unfaithful to your mom — I was also unfaithful to you. What I did many years ago by cheating on your mom with another woman was wrong. You did nothing to deserve it and neither did your mom. In fact, it really had nothing to do with you at all. It was all about me. I made it that way. In fact, I was so into me that after a while, I hardly noticed you or your mom at all. That's called selfishness and pride and I was eaten up with it. And even though God has been dealing with me in that area of my life ever since (and even before — I was just being rebellious and didn't realize it), I just wanted you to know how I felt and I am asking you for your forgiveness.

Secondly, I want you both to know how incredibly proud I am of you. I know we don't get to spend near as much time together as we used to or as we'd like to, but you are ALWAYS in my thoughts and I pray for you both all the time.

Chris, you're such a great guy and you have matured into a better man than I could have ever imagined. You've really risen up to the challenge these past several years and proven to me that you have what it takes to do whatever you want to in life. Don't ever underestimate the importance of honesty and integrity. I realize that when I failed you in that regard, God brought others into your life to show you what true integrity looks like. And while I will always regret that there were many years when I was not the man you could model yourself after, I'm thankful that God used that as well to further define your character.

Andrew, you are certainly Daddy's boy. God did something special when He molded your heart. So guard it and protect it, because others will always be out to steal it from you. This world we live in will never be a friendly place to a boy or a man with a heart like yours. But you don't have to live in fear as long as you remember to whom you belong. God has promised to never leave you and never forsake you, even to the end of time. Neither will I, although one day my time here on earth will end. You'll need to remind yourself that God is always with you, and know that I too am *ALWAYS* thinking of you and praying for you. The times we spend together are precious to me and I cherish every moment and memory. And if the past is any indicator, the years ahead will be even more exciting for us both. It may be harder to find the time to be together now that I live farther away, but it's always worth the effort when I do see you. You will always be worth it to me, both you and Chris.

For the past eleven years, I've been on a long road back to the heart of God. I committed my life to Him before you both were born, but failed over time to follow the example He gave me in Jesus Christ. When I was just a few years younger than you, Andrew, I saw pornography for the very first time. That was also the first of many, many secrets I would keep throughout my life regarding my sexuality and my sexual behaviors. The bottom line is I used to think of sex as a shameful, dirty thing. It certainly is portrayed that way in porn and in a lot of the movies and music in our culture, but that's not the way it really is. God created us as sexual beings and has always intended it to be a beautiful and powerful expression of the love between a man and a woman committed to each other and to Him in marriage. This is what I believe with all of my heart, so I hope you both come to believe it and understand it too. You really can trust God with everything, even your sexual desires. I had to learn the hard way that He's the only one who can be trusted with such a personal and powerful gift.

And so it is, a gift to us from God. I abused this gift for most of my life, and unfortunately because of my carelessness you both were hurt as was your mother and many other people. I think of the consequences of my sexual sins often, but most of all I'm reminded of our collective loss by the longing that remains in my heart to be with you both. I know you feel it too. Please don't forget where that pain we all feel came from. Because my greatest fear now as your father is that one of you will forget it or choose to ignore it, and if that happens you'll be destined to repeat my failings one day with your own wife and your own children. Generational sin works like that if we aren't careful and fail to guard our hearts. You both have each other and always will. Guard each other's hearts as well, and look out for each other's well-being, now and always.

You both have been through so much in your young lives, but you've also been so resilient and courageous. There's still a lot of life ahead of you, so cherish every moment of it. You've been a great inspiration to me as you have unselfishly allowed me to share our personal family story with so many others who struggle so they too can hope for better days ahead. Courageous acts like these are what God uses to build faith and character in those who love Him. So please don't forget to love God. Thank Him every day for the many blessings He has brought into your lives. Take time to talk to Him, and listen to what He has to say to you. Because whether you realize it or not, God is deeply interested and invested in your lives and has a plan that's ready and waiting for you. All you have to do is seek it out, seek God. You can trust Him and lean on Him and know that He has your best interests at heart. He knows your deepest desires as well as your biggest struggles and failings. You're bound to make mistakes in life, everyone does. But remember that He is always quick to forgive as long as your heart is repentant and your confession is true.

We never know how much time we have left on this earth. Chances are my time will expire long before yours, but that's not certain either. Just know that you both are loved more deeply by me than you could ever imagine. Not because of what you've done or where you've been, but because of who you are. You are my boys and you always will be.

With love always and forever,

Your Dad

CONCLUSION

HOW TO START
A REVOLUTION

A funny thing happened to me on my way to writing this book. I think I discovered a way to start a new sexual revolution.

It all came together while I was traveling in eastern Europe. I spoke at the University of Sarajevo in Bosnia. We had a standing-room-only crowd and the event went off without a hitch. Afterward, I hung out with some of the students and Campus Crusade for Christ staff who had attended the event. A couple of guys who stuck around started sharing about their experiences during the ethnic cleansing war and bloody siege of Sarajevo that lasted for several years. They were six and seven years old back then, like most of their peers attending the university. They explained that even today, early on in a relationship, two people would usually have a brief and superficial conversation about the war. Later, however, in order for the relationship to move into a deeper level of intimacy, they would often have the "big conversation" about what really went on and the suffering and battle scars that still remained in their own personal lives. They said that a lot of their day-to-day stress and tension and struggles came from being the children of war. Consequently, a lot of the guys there said that's also why they turned to porn—it was just another way for them to escape the pain. Yet even in the face of such insurmountable odds, their growing faith in Christ was giving them a newfound freedom they'd never experienced before.

Afterward, I was struck by the significance of what I had just heard. Reflecting on what I had shared that night during my talk with a few hundred students, I caught myself thinking, *Wow, if we could just find a way to take one of those students and train them on how to share their personal story with their peers. These students don't need to be listening to some older guy from a distant country and a different culture telling his story. How much more powerful for them to hear from one of their own about how their faith in God helped set them free from the power of porn in their life!*

> "I didn't like the part about God, 'cause I don't believe in Him."
>
> ~ COMMENT FROM A MALE STUDENT WHO ATTENDED PORN NATION IN BOSNIA

Later on that week I sat down with the campus ministry staff in Bosnia and Croatia and they challenged me to help them recruit, train, and equip one or two of their students in the coming year to do just that—to carry the message of the gospel of Jesus Christ to their peers back on campus through the power of their personal stories. They wanted me to help them raise up some of the first "new evangelists" of this kind in central Europe. So that's exactly what I plan on doing when I return next spring to Bosnia and Croatia, and when I visit Slovakia for the first time.

> "I liked the part about God, 'cause I also believe He can change everything."
>
> ~ COMMENT FROM A FEMALE STUDENT WHO ATTENDED PORN NATION IN CROATIA

Actually, the genesis of this new train of thought was much more gradual than it sounds. Since we've been using the online SAST for nearly four years now, this book has been writing itself through the survey results we've gotten and based on the interactions I've had with college students all over the world. As I've shared my personal story and experiences with the students, I've explained how pornography affects the body, mind, and soul. We've also talked about intimacy and the similarities between sexuality and spirituality—sexuality being about our intimacy with another human being and spirituality being about our pursuing intimacy with God. It seems that about 80 percent or more of our typical audience does not have a strong faith background or affiliation, but most are interested in spiritual things and they stick around for that part of the presentation that I always make "optional." Needless to say, our Q&A's at the end have been the source of some very spirited discussions.

> *"I have never known God and my family has never been religious. I would like to talk with someone about this."*
>
> ~ COMMENT FROM A FEMALE STUDENT WHO ATTENDED PORN NATION IN BOSNIA

While my student audiences have come across as sexually self-assured and confident in their sexual identities, our sex survey results reveal a very different story. Today's college students are soaking in a cesspool of sexual hype and imagery, and as a result, I believe it has left them feeling anything but confident about who they really are. Our findings have shown that a significant percentage of students are hiding their sexual behaviors as they struggle with sexual shame and guilt, while many others are fighting to maintain a sense of self-control in the face of growing sexual compulsivity. The message is loud and clear—things are not as great in our students' personal lives as they might want us to believe.

Yet I've also talked with many students who have shared how they've overcome their past struggles with body image issues, eating disorders, unwanted sexual behaviors, unhealthy relationships, even growing sexual addictions and addictions to porn. These students have had to dig much deeper into their souls and confront some soul-level issues that most others have worked hard to avoid. It's not uncommon to see these students make themselves available to others, including their peers, to offer them the help and hope they're missing. This new breed of student has the courage not

"Being an intelligent kid at a school with a lot of intelligent people, it's very easy to dismiss the existence of a God because science and education makes many people, myself included, feel like we can explain everything and make our own way. I haven't been to church in a while and I've lost touch with God. I can't say I've been completely overturned and my beliefs and opinions changed, but I am going to do some soul searching and pick up a Bible because of what I heard and saw tonight."

~ COMMENT FROM A MALE STUDENT WHO ATTENDED PORN NATION IN CROATIA

just to stand up and be counted but also to be counted on. Their credentials are found in their stories. For most, their story is the only thing they have, but it's often enough to help others in ways that nothing else can.

That is exactly why I believe the time is right for today's college students to rise up and start a new revolution, a sexual revolution, based on respect for the individual and God's design for sex, love, and relationships. I believe the leaders of this new sexual revolution will consist mainly of a large, emerging global contingent I refer to as the "new evangelists." These freedom fighters will come from every walk of life and every nationality and faith background, and each of their messages will be as unique as they are. Few will be seminary trained, yet all will speak of having a personal relationship with God through Jesus Christ that has in some way transformed their lives.

Each one will have a redemption story and will be the undisputed experts in their own accounts of coming back from debilitation. Not through preaching or apologetics (arguments in defense of Christian faith) but through the power of personal story, the lives of students around them will be changed. These new evangelists won't preach sermons but all will tell their stories and share with others about how their lives were transformed when they surrendered their lives to Christ. In their pursuit of sexual freedom, they discovered that the kind of intimacy they were really after was the kind of intimacy found only through a close connection with

God. Through this spiritual awakening, they then learned how to have healthier relationships with others, respecting boundaries and seeking out connections on a far deeper level than the shallowness of casual sex or the fantasies of porn could ever deliver.

While talk of a sexual revolution might sound like a bit of an exaggeration, the truth is nearly all the students I've spoken with at Porn University over the years tell me that they're growing tired of the sexual pressure that they constantly feel both on campus and off. Most acknowledge that for as long as they can remember, they've been immersed in an environment where pornographic, sexual images and messages have permeated their movies, music, TV shows, email, video game characters, chat rooms, text messages, and even casual conversations with friends. To hear some of them talk about it and speak of wanting to do something about it is to see the emergence of a new kind of student with the heart and soul and passion of a revolutionary. The cause couldn't be more important as without it, their younger brothers and sisters and maybe even their own children are likely to suffer far greater consequences than they ever will. These students will face stiff opposition from a mammoth global industry and many who still see porn as a harmless form of entertainment. But in the end I believe they'll carry the day as others who can identify with their story will emerge to join

> *"I've had religious stuff shoved down my throat for years, but the true gospel message finally spoke to me through Michael's story as a true message of love and personal relationship."*
>
> ~ COMMENT FROM A FEMALE COLLEGE STUDENT WHO PRAYED TO RECEIVE CHRIST AT A PORN NATION EVENT

> *"This speech caused two important realizations for me: First, I saw pornography as yet another way for corporations to control us. Second, for the first time, I began to consider Christianity as a real option for my life. I haven't decided yet, but I would like to learn more."*
>
> ~ COMMENT FROM A MALE COLLEGE STUDENT

"God does not solve all problems. Man needs to solve it by himself, or with others, and not with God."

~ COMMENT FROM A MALE
STUDENT WHO ATTENDED
PORN NATION IN CROATIA

"Right now, I am not sure which one is greater evil— the pornography or the religion???"

~ COMMENT FROM A MALE
STUDENT WHO ATTENDED
PORN NATION IN BOSNIA

"I cried. Very emotional. I felt more of a connection with God. I really want to change. I hope it sticks with me. Thank you."

~ COMMENT FROM A FEMALE
COLLEGE STUDENT

the movement, driven by their own desire to experience the true sexual freedom that has eluded them for so long.

What about you? If you are a parent reading this book, you can join the revolution too. There will be many jobs that need to get done and many tasks to complete. The first and foremost is being there for your kids and becoming the kind of parent they need you to be. This will require healing old wounds of your own, and reconciling and restoring broken relationships—for their sake if for no other reason. The same goes for grandparents and family and friends as well as others who work with students. Everyone can help make this far-fetched dream a reality. But most of all, this revolution belongs to today's college student. If that's you, then it's yours for the taking if you're finally fed up with the status quo and ready to change the world the way that God is changing you.

It will be no easy task. And the road you'll travel is sure to be fraught with doubters and skeptics, especially among many of your peers still hanging out and following the crowd at Porn University. So what do you think? Are you ready to start a revolution? If so, then contact us and let us know today. Because there are millions of people in the world literally dying to hear your story. Our website is www.bravehearts.net and you can email us at mleahy@bravehearts.net.

APPENDIX

SAST SURVEY RESULTS

Note: Since not all respondents chose to answer every question, the total number of respondents, as well as totals for male and female responses, will vary from question to question.

Which college do you attend? (If your school isn't listed, check Other and specify)

COLLEGE	TOTAL SURVEYS		MALE		FEMALE	
University of Wisconsin-Madison	2133	30.50%	1041	26.04%	1115	37.17%
Purdue University	2011	24.67%	1450	28.97%	604	18.92%
Indiana University	1179	16.86%	663	16.58%	513	17.10%
UC Davis	1023	14.40%	554	14.18%	466	14.74%
University of Southern California	915	11.23%	528	10.55%	384	12.03%
Northern Illinois University	824	10.11%	467	9.33%	359	11.24%
University of North Carolina-Chapel Hill	747	9.16%	371	7.41%	374	11.71%
UC Santa Barbara	743	10.46%	374	9.57%	367	11.61%
University of Washington	619	8.71%	376	9.62%	239	7.56%
Northwestern University	613	8.63%	342	8.75%	268	8.48%
Michigan State University	603	9.97%	396	10.73%	203	8.73%
Iowa State University	559	9.24%	403	10.92%	155	6.67%
New Mexico State University	546	9.03%	310	8.40%	235	10.11%
Brown University	495	8.18%	278	7.54%	213	9.16%
Marshall University	479	7.92%	242	6.56%	232	9.98%
Univ of South Florida	459	5.63%	256	5.11%	202	6.33%
SUNY at Buffalo	409	5.76%	264	6.76%	145	4.59%
Univ of Saskatchewan	384	6.35%	205	5.56%	177	7.61%
Oregon State University	381	6.30%	224	6.07%	155	6.67%
Univ of Tampa	370	4.54%	170	3.40%	198	6.20%
Kansas State University	339	5.60%	224	6.07%	114	4.90%
UC Irvine	332	4.75%	205	5.13%	132	4.40%
Northeastern	313	3.84%	171	3.42%	142	4.45%
Mississippi State University	296	4.17%	181	4.63%	114	3.61%
University of Michigan	276	3.95%	138	3.45%	136	4.53%
University of North Florida	248	3.49%	148	3.79%	97	3.07%

COLLEGE	TOTAL SURVEYS		MALE		FEMALE	
University of South Carolina-Aiken	245	4.05%	101	2.74%	143	6.15%
Kennesaw State University	244	3.43%	135	3.46%	108	3.42%
Michigan Tech	236	3.37%	167	4.18%	68	2.27%
Wittenberg University	233	3.28%	73	1.87%	160	5.06%
Texas Christian University	228	2.80%	128	2.56%	99	3.10%
University of North Dakota	221	3.11%	138	3.53%	83	2.62%
Western Washington University	218	3.07%	113	2.89%	103	3.26%
Denison University	197	2.77%	71	1.82%	125	3.95%
University of Nebraska-Lincoln	183	2.58%	96	2.46%	85	2.69%
Eastern Michigan University	176	2.52%	74	1.85%	101	3.37%
West Chester University	161	1.98%	71	1.42%	88	2.76%
University of Memphis	145	2.07%	110	2.75%	35	1.17%
IUPU-Indianapolis	138	1.94%	64	1.64%	74	2.34%
Wabash College	134	2.22%	126	3.42%	8	0.34%
Boston U	131	1.61%	74	1.48%	56	1.75%
University of Oregon	130	1.83%	72	1.84%	55	1.74%
Jacksonville University	126	1.77%	82	2.10%	43	1.36%
University of Wisconsin-Eau Claire	125	1.79%	72	1.80%	53	1.77%
Indiana University-South Bend	122	1.72%	74	1.89%	48	1.52%
IIT	119	1.46%	97	1.94%	23	0.72%
University of Calgary	114	1.88%	66	1.79%	47	2.02%
Emory University	109	1.53%	57	1.46%	52	1.64%
Dickinson State University	97	1.60%	51	1.38%	46	1.98%
Indiana State University	97	1.37%	47	1.20%	50	1.58%
Ripon College	92	1.52%	31	0.84%	61	2.62%
Case Western Reserve University	91	1.30%	57	1.43%	34	1.13%
University of Illinois at Chicago	87	1.07%	59	1.18%	28	0.88%
Marquette University	84	1.39%	37	1.00%	47	2.02%
Western Oregon University	84	1.39%	38	1.03%	45	1.94%
University of Idaho	82	1.17%	45	1.13%	37	1.23%
University of Kansas	75	1.07%	42	1.05%	30	1.00%
Columbia College	71	0.87%	34	0.68%	37	1.16%
University of Alberta	68	1.12%	44	1.19%	23	0.99%
University of Chicago	64	0.79%	45	0.90%	17	0.53%
University of Wisconsin La Crosse	60	0.84%	21	0.54%	38	1.20%
Loyola	58	0.71%	30	0.60%	27	0.85%
Cal Poly Pomona	55	0.77%	41	1.05%	13	0.41%
Carleton University	55	0.79%	40	1.00%	15	0.50%
University of North Carolina -Wilmington	55	0.67%	28	0.56%	24	0.75%
Southwestern Oklahoma State University	54	0.77%	36	0.90%	17	0.57%
University of Central Oklahoma (UCO)	52	0.74%	25	0.63%	31	1.03%
Georgia Tech	37	0.52%	29	0.74%	8	0.25%
College of Lake County	34	0.42%	23	0.46%	10	0.31%

COLLEGE	TOTAL SURVEYS		MALE		FEMALE	
Roosevelt (IL)	32	0.39%	13	0.26%	19	0.60%
Northern Michigan University	28	0.40%	17	0.43%	11	0.37%
University of Ottawa	23	0.33%	11	0.28%	11	0.37%
George Mason University	20	0.25%	10	0.20%	10	0.31%
University of Wisconsin-Milwaukee	19	0.31%	11	0.30%	8	0.34%
Bellevue Community College	17	0.24%	11	0.28%	6	0.19%
Mount Union College	16	0.23%	10	0.25%	5	0.17%
Butler University	15	0.21%	7	0.18%	8	0.25%
East Central University (ECU)	15	0.21%	10	0.25%	5	0.17%
West Chester University	15	0.21%	7	0.18%	8	0.25%
Youngstown State University	12	0.17%	8	0.20%	3	0.10%
Penn State-Altoona	10	0.17%	7	0.19%	3	0.13%
U Mass Boston	10	0.12%	5	0.10%	5	0.16%
Cleveland State University	9	0.13%	6	0.15%	2	0.07%
Colleges of the Fenway	9	0.11%	4	0.08%	5	0.16%
Limestone College	9	0.13%	5	0.13%	4	0.13%
Chicago School of Arts Institute	8	0.10%	6	0.12%	2	0.06%
East Tennessee State University	8	0.11%	5	0.13%	2	0.06%
University of Zagreeb	8	0.11%	8	0.20%	0	0.00%
Belhaven College	6	0.07%	2	0.04%	4	0.13%
Milwaukee Area Tech College	6	0.10%	4	0.11%	1	0.04%
New Mexico State University	6	0.08%	4	0.10%	2	0.06%
Univ of Wisconsin-Parkside	6	0.10%	3	0.08%	2	0.09%
Univ of Tennessee-Martin	5	0.07%	4	0.10%	1	0.03%
Fort Lewis College	4	0.05%	3	0.06%	1	0.03%
Johnson County Community College (MO)	4	0.05%	3	0.06%	1	0.03%
Minot State University	4	0.07%	2	0.05%	2	0.09%
Baldwin Wallace College	3	0.04%	3	0.08%	0	0.00%
Eckerd College	3	0.05%	2	0.05%	1	0.04%
Georgia State University	3	0.04%	1	0.03%	2	0.06%
Missouri Western State University	3	0.04%	3	0.06%	0	0.00%
University of Missouri-Kansas City	3	0.04%	3	0.06%	0	0.00%
University of Rijeka	3	0.04%	1	0.03%	1	0.03%
University of Split	3	0.04%	3	0.08%	0	0.00%
Valpariso University	3	0.04%	1	0.03%	2	0.06%
University of Mass-Dartmouth	2	0.03%	2	0.05%	0	0.00%
University of Sarajevo	2	0.03%	2	0.05%	0	0.00%
University of Wisconsin-Whitewater	2	0.03%	2	0.05%	0	0.00%
Other (specify)	1405	17.24%	952	19.02%	474	14.84%
Other (specify)	917	12.91%	519	13.28%	391	12.37%
Other	1295	21.41%	882	23.91%	404	17.38%
Other	1844	26.37%	1193	29.84%	640	21.33%
Total	**6993**		**3998**		**3000**	

	TOTAL SURVEYS		MALE		FEMALE	
What is your gender?						
Male	16896	59%				
Female	11762	41%				
Total	**28715**		**16988**		**11810**	
Year in school or occupation?						
Freshman	7919	28%	4375	26%	3625	31%
Sophomore	5915	21%	3329	20%	2587	22%
Junior	5403	19%	3047	18%	2351	20%
Senior	4956	17%	2931	17%	2005	17%
Postgraduate	2156	8%	1512	9%	637	5%
Faculty	178	1%	141	1%	36	0%
Administration / staff	470	2%	325	2%	143	1%
Other (specify)	1518	4%	1112	7%	390	3%
Total	**28515**		**16772**		**11774**	
What is your age?						
18-21	19889	70%	10840		9122	
22-25	5290	19%	3428		1845	
Over 25	2965	10%	2305		644	
Under 18	295	1%	177		26	
Total	**28439**		**16750**		**11637**	
Approximately how old were you when you first viewed pornography (sexually explicit material)?						
5 yrs. or younger	510	2%	318	2%	185	2%
6	345	1%	227	1%	117	1%
7	552	2%	348	2%	204	2%
8	940	3%	620	4%	315	3%
9	869	3%	589	4%	286	3%
10	2285	8%	1614	10%	659	6%
11	2107	7%	1569	9%	565	5%
12	4386	16%	3202	19%	1160	10%
13	4164	15%	2981	18%	1183	10%
14	3397	12%	2237	13%	1158	10%
15	2380	8%	1352	8%	1040	9%
16 yrs. or older	6190	22%	1742	10%	4466	39%
Total	**28125**		**16799**		**11338**	

	TOTAL SURVEYS	MALE	FEMALE
What form of pornography were you exposed to that first time?			
Internet or computer-based (photos or video)	9785 35%	5869 35%	3935 35%
Soft or hard-core print magazines	8809 32%	6523 39%	2292 20%
Soft or hard-core VHS or DVD movies	3742 13%	1719 10%	2019 18%
Cable TV or pay-per-view	4909 18%	2236 13%	2661 24%
Other (specify)	647 2%	268 2%	370 3%
Total	**27892**	**16615**	**11277**

	TOTAL SURVEYS	MALE	FEMALE
How many hours do you spend online per week?			
Less than 5	2915 10%	1635 10%	1263 11%
5-20	15274 54%	8698 52%	6582 57%
21-50	8169 29%	5080 30%	3105 27%
Over 50	2027 7%	1349 8%	681 6%
Total	**28385**	**16762**	**11631**

	TOTAL SURVEYS	MALE	FEMALE
How many hours do you spend online for Internet sex per week?			
0	15580 55%	6091 36%	9523 82%
Less than 5	10362 37%	8523 51%	1837 16%
5-20	1994 7%	1814 11%	165 1%
Over 20	368 1%	285 2%	70 1%
Total	**28304**	**16713**	**11595**

	TOTAL SURVEYS	MALE	FEMALE

1. Were you sexually abused as a child or adolescent?

Yes	2353	8%	901	5%	1423	12%
No	26304	92%	15924	95%	10291	88%
Total	**28657**		**16825**		**11714**	

2. Do you regularly read romance novels or sexually explicit magazines, or regularly visit sexually explicit web sites or chat rooms?

Yes	9450	33%	7065	42%	2292	20%
No	19201	67%	9753	58%	9428	80%
Total	**28651**		**16818**		**11720**	

3. Have you stayed in romantic relationships after they become emotionally or physically abusive?

Yes	4393	15%	1735	10%	2650	23%
No	24185	85%	15036	90%	9053	77%
Total	**28578**		**16771**		**11703**	

4. Do you often find yourself preoccupied with sexual thoughts or romantic daydreams?

Yes	18687	65%	11368	68%	7226	62%
No	9939	35%	5442	32%	4483	38%
Total	**28626**		**16810**		**11709**	

5. Do you feel that your sexual behavior is not normal?

Yes	5395	19%	3541	21%	1787	15%
No	23192	81%	13246	79%	9907	85%
Total	**28587**		**16787**		**11694**	

6. Does your spouse (or significant other(s)) ever worry or complain about your sexual behavior?

Yes	2483	9%	1637	10%	814	7%
No	26017	91%	15097	90%	10848	93%
Total	**28500**		**16734**		**11662**	

	TOTAL SURVEYS		MALE		FEMALE	

7. Do you have trouble stopping your sexual behavior when you know it is inappropriate?

Yes	6436	23%	4279	26%	2111	18%
No	22129	77%	12488	74%	9581	82%
Total	28565		16767		11692	

8. Do you ever feel bad about your sexual behavior?

Yes	11960	42%	7337	44%	4553	39%
No	16556	58%	9408	56%	7112	61%
Total	28516		16745		11665	

9. Has your sexual behavior ever created problems for you and your family or friends?

Yes	4632	16%	2930	18%	1683	14%
No	23826	84%	13778	82%	9963	86%
Total	28458		16708		11646	

10. Have you ever sought help for sexual behavior you did not like?

Yes	1913	7%	1424	9%	469	4%
No	26512	93%	15267	91%	11165	96%
Total	28425		16691		11634	

11. Have you ever worried about people finding out about your sexual activities?

Yes	14685	52%	8848	53%	5783	50%
No	13768	48%	7848	47%	5871	50%
Total	28453		16696		11654	

12. Has anyone been hurt emotionally because of your sexual behavior?

Yes	12506	44%	7586	45%	4860	42%
No	15946	56%	9108	55%	6797	58%
Total	28452		16694		11657	

13. Have you ever participated in sexual activity in exchange for money or gifts?

Yes	1399	8%	995	9%	377	5%
No	17198	92%	9825	91%	7328	95%
Total	18597		10820		7705	

	TOTAL SURVEYS		MALE		FEMALE	

14. Do you have times when you act out sexually followed by periods of celibacy (no sex at all)?

Yes	7865	28%	4476	27%	3361	29%
No	20524	72%	12165	73%	8285	71%
Total	28389		16641		11646	

15. Have you made efforts to quit a type of sexual activity and failed?

Yes	9072	32%	6324	38%	2672	23%
No	19339	68%	10360	62%	8956	77%
Total	28411		16684		11628	

16. Do you hide some of your sexual behavior from others?

Yes	15692	55%	9596	58%	6037	52%
No	12703	45%	7061	42%	5603	48%
Total	28395		16657		11640	

17. Do you find yourself having multiple romantic relationships at the same time?

Yes	3826	13%	2275	14%	1525	13%
No	24546	87%	14361	86%	10114	87%
Total	28372		16636		11639	

18. Have you ever felt degraded by your sexual behavior?

Yes	8704	31%	4817	29%	3861	33%
No	19680	69%	11839	71%	7769	67%
Total	28384		16656		11630	

19. Has sex or romantic fantasies been a way for you to escape your problems?

Yes	8876	31%	5469	33%	3349	29%
No	19481	69%	11171	67%	8268	71%
Total	28357		16640		11617	

20. When you have sex, do you feel depressed afterwards?

Yes	3310	12%	1907	11%	1370	12%
No	24948	88%	14676	89%	10205	88%
Total	28258		16583		11575	

	TOTAL SURVEYS	MALE	FEMALE

21. Do you regularly engage in sadomasochistic behavior (S&M, i.e., sex with whips, leather, spanking, pain, etc.)?

Yes	1865	7%	866	5%	989	8%
No	26534	93%	15795	95%	10652	92%
Total	28399		16661		11641	

22. Has your sexual activity interfered with your family life?

Yes	1617	6%	1117	7%	490	4%
No	26766	94%	15537	93%	11141	96%
Total	28383		16654		11631	

23. Have you been sexual with minors?

Yes	2766	10%	2162	13%	606	5%
No	25593	90%	14486	87%	11001	95%
Total	28359		16648		11607	

24. Do you feel controlled by your sexual desire or fantasies of romance?

Yes	4346	15%	3187	19%	1135	10%
No	23951	85%	13413	81%	10462	90%
Total	28297		16600		11597	

25. Do you ever think your sexual desire is stronger than you are?

Yes	6050	21%	4292	26%	1719	15%
No	22290	79%	12344	74%	9884	85%
Total	28340		16636		11603	

INTRODUCTION

1. The following are books I recommend that explore the relationship between sexuality and spirituality. *Sex God: Exploring the Endless Connections between Sexuality and Spirituality* by Rob Bell, Zondervan, 2007; *False Intimacy: Understanding the Struggle of Sexual Addiction* by Harry Schaumburg, NavPress, 1997; *Sex and the Supremacy of Christ* by John Piper, Crossway Books, 2005.

CHAPTER 1: BACK TO SCHOOL

1. The terms "compulsive" and "addictive" are frequently used together to characterize those who suffer from addictions. Compulsion refers to strong impulses to act a certain way, and addiction refers to the particular behaviors that the addict engages in to satisfy his or her compulsive thoughts.

CHAPTER 7: SEX ON THE BRAIN

1. Shaunti Feldhahn, *For Women Only* (Sisters, OR: Multnomah, 2004), 111.
2. Ibid., 116.
3. Ibid., 112.

CHAPTER 8: SO HOW'S THAT WORKING FOR YOU?

1. *The American Heritage Dictionary of the English Language*, 4th ed. (Boston: Houghton Mifflin, 2006).

CHAPTER 9: WHO'S IN CONTROL HERE?

1. Dr. Patrick Carnes favors the lower end of the estimate, placing it between 3 and 6%. See SexHelp.com, "Frequently Asked Questions," http://www.sexhelp.com/addiction_faq.cfm#how-many. Alvin Cooper et al. place the estimate higher. See Alvin Cooper, Dana E. Putnam, Lynn A. Planchon, and Sylvain C. Boies, "Online Sexual Compulsivity: Getting Tangled in the Net," *Sexual Addiction and Compulsivity* 6:2 (1999): 79–104.

2. See Lauren Slater, "'True Love: Scientists Say That the Brain Chemistry of Infatuation Is Akin to Mental Illness—Which Gives New Meaning to 'Madly in Love,'" *National Geographic*, February 2006, 32–50.

CHAPTER 10: FROM SEX SYNDROME TO SEX ADDICTION

1. Alvin Cooper, Dana E. Putnam, Lynn A. Planchon, and Sylvain C. Boies, "Online Sexual Compulsivity: Getting Tangled in the Net," *Sexual Addiction and Compulsivity* 6:2 (1999): 79–104.

2. Dr. Patrick Carnes, SexHelp.com, "Important Definitions," http://www.sexhelp.com/addiction_definitions.cfm.

3. Michael Herkov, Ph.D., "What Is Sexual Addiction?" *Psych Central*, December 10, 2006, http://psychcentral.com/lib/2006/what-is-sexual-addiction.

4. Mayo Clinic Staff, "Compulsive Sexual Behavior," MayoClinic.com Health Library, September 29, 2005, http://www.riversideonline.com/health_reference/Behavior-Mental-Health/DS00144.cfm.

5. Dr. Patrick Carnes, SexHelp.com, "Frequently Asked Questions," http://www.sexhelp.com/addiction_faq.cfm#how-many.

6. Alvin Cooper, Dana E. Putnam, Lynn A. Planchon, and Sylvain C. Boies, "Online Sexual Compulsivity: Getting Tangled in the Net," *Sexual Addiction and Compulsivity* 6:2 (1999): 79–104.

7. Dr. Patrick Carnes, "Frequently Asked Questions," http://www.sexhelp.com/addiction_faq.cfm#multiple.

8. Dr. Patrick Carnes, "Frequently Asked Questions," http://www.sexhelp.com/addiction_faq.cfm#male-female.

9. Dr. Patrick Carnes, "Frequently Asked Questions," http://www.sexhelp.com/addiction_faq.cfm#behavior.

10. See Patrick Carnes, *Out of the Shadows: Understanding Sexual Addiction* (Center City, MN: Hazelden, 1992), 99–102.

ACKNOWLEDGMENTS

Having written my third book, it's easier to see how so many people, places, and past experiences go into the completion of such large writing projects. There are those who influence every such endeavor, and others whose contributions are more closely tied to one particular work. I'd like to acknowledge both here.

First and foremost, thanks to my good friends and their families at Campus Crusade for Christ. Without your partnership and your passion for reaching every student, this book would not have been possible. Special thanks always to Nick DeCola, Tony Arnold, and Rick James, my three amigos and charter members of "The Band." Also, to Bob Francis, Jim Topmiller, Tom Goodwin, Brooke Butler, Jim Kelly, and Derrick Grow, thanks for trusting me and for all of the "firsts" you represent as true pioneers in our partnerships. I'd also like to thank Mark Gauthier, Marc Rutter, Dan Hardaway, Keith Davy, Larry Stephens, Dennis Brockman, Laurie Menefee, and the countless other staff and local level leaders too numerous to mention here who have inspired me with their dedicated and selfless service to college students throughout the world.

Many thanks as usual to David Sanford, Elizabeth Jones, and the rest of the team at Credo Communications, Inc., as well as to Andy McGuire, Randall Payleitner, and the rest of the team at Moody Publishers for your support, encouragement, and assistance in making this book a reality. You are all amazing!

To my brothers and sisters Cathy, Tim, June, Joe, and their families, thank you for your ongoing love and support. And especially my mom, aka "Mona." You have always been my best friend and an encouragement to me, but especially in my efforts to connect with college students by sharing our family history and my personal message of hope and help. I love it that you still let me be your buddy and the baby of the family, even at fifty. And to my boys, to whom this book is dedicated, and their mom, who has invested her entire life teaching students and inspiring them to make a difference in this world, thank you for your loving encouragement and support of my ministry and me.

And finally to my beautiful bride, Christine. Once again, you've suffered through countless late night and weekend writing marathons, endured the drama of meeting publisher deadlines, and tolerated the sight of me lounging around the house all summer long writing while wearing pretty much the same shirts and gym shorts, "my uniform." Yet long before we first met at that Porn Nation event in Chicago, you had dedicated your life to working with college students, helping them navigate their way through the chaos of campus life. I've learned so much from you about today's students, and gained insights I could have never hoped to find on my own. Thank you for loving me through it all and pushing me to be so much more than I ever envisioned God wanted me to be.

ABOUT THE AUTHOR

Michael Leahy is a recovering sex addict and the founder and executive director of BraveHearts, an organization dedicated to increasing the public's awareness of the hidden dangers and long-term consequences of pornography consumption. Before launching BraveHearts in 2002, Michael was a sales executive in the computer industry and worked for companies like IBM, Unisys, and NEC. Michael is the father of two boys, Chris and Andrew; his first marriage ended in divorce in 1998 after his thirty-year relationship with pornography escalated into an affair resulting from a self-destructive sexual addiction.

Now ten years into recovery, Michael has appeared on numerous national television programs like ABC's *20/20* and *The View* and in major media publications such as *USA Today* as an expert on the subjects of pornography, sexual addiction, and the impact sex in media is having on our culture. He's shared his compelling story and expertise in churches, at conferences, and with over one hundred thousand students on more than one hundred fifty college campuses worldwide in his critically acclaimed, multimedia-intensive live-speaker presentation called "Porn Nation: The Naked Truth." Michael is remarried and currently resides with his wife, Christine, in the Washington, DC area.

PORN NATION

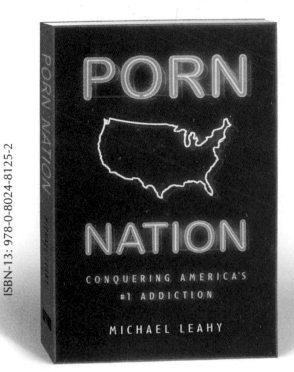

ISBN-13: 978-0-8024-8125-2

Pornography and sex-related sites make up nearly 60 percent of daily web traffic. For some of us, it's going on in our very own basements or in the den after the family goes to bed. Over twenty million Americans spend a good deal of their waking hours looking at pornography. And they won't stop, because they can't stop. At least not on their own. They are addicted. But it's also the story of the rest of us. It's the story of America – our porn nation. How is it affecting us? How is it changing the way we see ourselves and others? And what can be done about it?

NORTHFIELD
PUBLISHING

1-800-678-8812 • MOODYPUBLISHERS.COM

PORN @ WORK

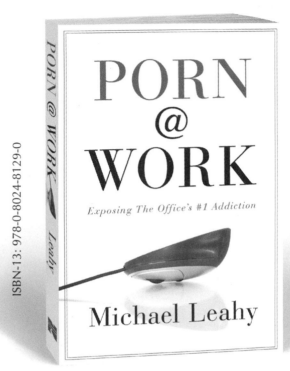

ISBN-13: 978-0-8024-8129-0

Speaking from personal experience and drawing on several years' worth of research surveys, author Michael Leahy presents the facts about our porn-saturated world in the place where we spend the most time: our jobs. The latest era of workplace connectivity has led to a whole new level of office efficiency, but it has also opened the door to all kinds of potential dangers and temptations. Lost productivity and litigation risks are where the errant click-throughs generally lead.
Don't fall into the trap! Porn doesn't have to be the norm.

1-800-678-8812 • MOODYPUBLISHERS.COM